HUMMER H2

JOHN LAMM &
MATT DELORENZO

MOTORBOOKS
INTERNATIONAL

First published in 2002 by Motorbooks International, Galtier Plaza, Suite 200, 380 Jackson Street, St. Paul, MN 55101-3885 USA

Motorbooks International titles are also available at discounts in bulk quantity for industrial or sales-promotional use. For details write to Special Sales Manager at Motorbooks International Wholesalers & Distributors, Galtier Plaza, Suite 200, 380 Jackson Street, St. Paul, MN 55101-3885 USA.

Library of Congress Cataloging-in-Publication Data Available

ISBN 0-7603-1244-3

On the front cover: The H2 is a capable off-road rig, and can handle two feet of water with aplomb. *General Motors*

On the frontispiece: Each Hummer's rugged body has been designed for high structural rigidity, which not only adds to its off-road abilities but also virtually eliminates squeaks and rattles during normal driving. *General Motors*

On the title page: Given the enthusiasm for the Hummer H1 and H2, it's apparent that there is a golden future ahead for the products of this unusual corporate tie-up between GM and AM General. *John Lamm*

On the back cover: The Hummer H2 concept vehicle photographed outside the styling dome at the automaker's huge design center. *General Motors*

Edited by Lee Klancher
Designed by Todd Westover

Printed in China

CONTENTS

ACKNOWLEDGMENTS

THIS INSIDE LOOK INTO THE DEVELOPMENT OF the Hummer H2 is a joint effort in every sense of the word between John Lamm and myself. In addition to photographing the H2 on a cross-country trip from Michigan to California, John researched and wrote the chapter on the history of AM General and the Hummer H1 and all the caption material.

Access is the key to success in any book that endeavors to tell the inside story, and we're most grateful to General Motors and AM General for their cooperation.

In particular, our gratitude goes to Sharon Basel of GM's Lifecycle Production Communications team for setting up interviews, arranging vehicles, and obtaining photos and illustrations used in this book. At AM General, PR Director Craig McNabb was instrumental in arranging a plant tour with company president and CEO Jim Armour, who generously gave up the afternoon as our tour guide and host.

Equally generous with their time were Project Manager Ken Lindensmith, GM Designer Clay Dean, as well as Hummer General Manager Mike DiGiovanni and Marketing Manager Marc Hernandez. We'd also like to thank Hummer communications staffers Wendy Orthman, Heather Hall, and Alan Adler. A special thanks goes out to photographer Jim Fets for additional images of the H2 in action.

Finally, we'd like to thank our families for their support John's wife Scheri, and daughter, Holly, and my wife, Jane, and our children, Amy and Stephen.

—*Matt DeLorenzo*

INTRODUCTION

THERE ARE FEW VEHICLES THAT HAVE THE EYE-catching presence of a Hummer. It's been a larger-than-life, genuine war hero through its service in the Gulf War. The civilian version is considered the ultimate in hip rides by the Hollywood set. It can stop dead in their tracks a playground full of kids.

Hummers are cool.

Obviously it's a vehicle with great mass appeal. But until recently, only 3,000 or so Hummers per year at over $100,000 each have made it onto the civilian market.

The Hummer H2, at less than half the price, is expected to tap into that enthusiasm and will set the stage for other even more affordable Hummers to come.

Not since Jeep successfully made the transition to the civilian market after the end of World War II has a military vehicle maker joined the ranks of mainstream automotive marketers.

So the Hummer H2 is not only the birth of a new vehicle, it is the beginning of a new kind of vehicle company that teams one of the largest manufacturers in the world, General Motors, with one of the smallest, AM General.

It is a remarkable story on many different levels—the unique arrangement where GM has acquired the Hummer brand name, while AM General builds the vehicles. The H2 itself uses many components from existing GM full-size SUVs and yet through the design and engineering process, a vehicle has emerged that is unmistakably a Hummer in appearance and, most important, capability.

Above all, it's a tale of the amazing speed with which events unfolded. GM began initial negotiations with AM General in the spring of 1999, signing the formal agreement at the end of the year. The Hummer H2 concept was revealed in January 2000 at the North American International Auto Show. In less than 30 months, customers were taking delivery of Hummer H2s built at a brand-new state-of-the-art manufacturing plant at AM General headquarters in Mishawaka, Ind. In less time than it takes the industry to do a makeover of an existing vehicle, GM and AM General conceived, developed, and put in place the capacity to build 40,000 all-new Hummer H2s.

Like the vehicle itself, the story of how the Hummer H2 came to be goes places never thought possible. It begins where the road ends.

HUMMER ORIGINS

ALTHOUGH THE HUMMER H1 HAS A ROCK-SOLID REPUTA-TION AS A GO-ANYWHERE, CLIMB-A-WALL, HE-MAN MACHINE, ITS HISTORIC ROOTS RUN BACK A CENTURY TO A SPINDLY HORSELESS CARRIAGE CALLED THE OVERLAND RUNABOUT.

Much of the company genealogy through the first four decades of the twentieth century is not particularly memorable. It includes such tidbits as becoming the Willys-Overland Company; producing the Willys-Knight with its interesting, if faulted, Knight sleeve-valve engine; creating a car called the Whippet; bankruptcy; and reorganization during the Depression. The firm survived and arrived on the doorstep of World War II with a design for a new 1/4-ton utility truck that became legend. The Willys-Overland Jeep is one of the most notable vehicle icons of the century, with the company producing some 350,000 for military services.

DaimlerChrysler now owns the Jeep name and the machine's general consumer popularity is obvious, but it wasn't apparent in the first decades after the war as the company struggled along with such models as the Jeepster.

In 1953 Willys-Overland became Willys Motors then the Kaiser Jeep Corporation a decade later. The company's showrooms weren't successful and you didn't see a lot of Jeeps in parking lots, but Kaiser was profitable thanks to contracts to build such recognizable non-consumer vehicles as the second-generation military "jeep," the M151; scores of 1 1/4-ton trucks for the armed services; and thousands of vehicles that reliably delivered the mail throughout the United States each day. It was an unglamorous but profitable history.

In 1970 American Motors Corporation (AMC) thought enough of the company to buy the Kaiser Jeep Corporation. A year later it split off a portion of the company, the Defense and Government Products Division, into a new corporate entity called AM General Corporation.

This is where the tree divides. The Jeep branch became consumer driven, and AM General continued with government work, creating everything from buses and dump trucks to more military vehicles.

It was one of these contracts with the government that led to a replacement for the M151 military "Jeep." In 1979

The great grandfather of all Hummers is the famous Willys World War II Jeep, which was known throughout the world for its go-anywhere, four-wheel drive versatility and ruggedness. *John Lamm*

AM General started the basic work on the M998 series High Mobility Multi-Purpose Wheeled Vehicle, designated the HMMWV. The name was militarized to "Humvee" and later civilianized to "Hummer."

AMC, trying to raise cash to stave off what would be its inevitable doom as an automaker, sold off AM General to LTV Corporation in 1983. American Motors lost the battle to stay independent and was bought out by Chrysler in 1987. Chrysler was then taken over 11 years later by Daimler-Benz and incorporated into DaimlerChrysler.

In 1992 LTV sold AM General to a New York company called Renco Group Inc., which retained the AM General name. Seven years later, General Motors (GM)—looking to broaden its share of the sport-utility vehicle (SUV) market—bought the brand name

AM General civilianized the military Humvee and created the H1, keeping the big machine's unique proportions and making little compromise for street life. *John Lamm*

"Hummer" from AM General. Under the agreement, GM would take over the marketing of the original Hummer, the H1 model, and develop a new, smaller version called the H2, the subject of this book. To understand why GM paid big money for the Hummer rights (the company won't say how much), we need to backtrack to 1979 and the early plans for what would become the Humvee.

Any Vietnam veteran schooled in the fundamentals of driving the M151 "Jeep" probably recalls the cautions given about how not to drive it. Because of the machine's all-wheel swing-axle independent suspension, it had a

Hummer H1s have been sold in a variety of body styles, for two or four passengers, enclosed or with a pickup bed, and with prices up to and over $100,000. *John Lamm*

tendency to tip over. It could be dangerous, as could another utility stalwart, the 1/4-ton "Mule"—both great ideas on paper that didn't work out that well when placed in the field.

To replace the M151, the Mule and several other vehicles in its inventory, the Army wanted a single, rugged, all-purpose platform that could be configured as anything from a pickup truck to an ambulance to a mobile machine-gun carrier. This single-platform strategy would mean a common vehicle, parts and technical know-how for a variety of uses, rather than a variety of machines purpose-built for different uses where each type

Like their military counterparts, a 6.5-liter GM V-8 turbo diesel powers the Hummer H1. Ratings for the big engine are 195 horsepower and an impressive 430 foot-pounds of torque. *John Lamm*

of vehicle needed its own stock of parts and specially trained mechanics. Plans for this new vehicle called for it to be reasonably lightweight and compact so it could be packed into cargo planes or hauled around by helicopters.

A pretty tall order, but right up AM General's technical alley.

Work on the Humvee design began in 1979; the contract to develop the prototypes was granted two years later. During five months in 1982, development and operations trials were held, and the Army was impressed enough that in March 1983 AM General won a $1.2 billion contract to produce an initial batch of 55,000 units over five years.

Although reworked for civilian life, the cockpit of a Hummer H1 still retains the feeling of a military vehicle, with no-nonsense gauges and controls spread across the instrument panel. *John Lamm*

Thanks to the versatility of the design, that first contract covered one platform, but five fundamental models done in 15 configurations.

That was only a start, because the military came back for more Humvees, and the machine so impressed America's allies that more than 30 of them also placed

orders for Humvees. Before the end of 2000, more than 150,000 Humvees had been delivered for service to the U.S. Armed Forces and other country's militaries.

For several years most Americans knew little about this amazing military vehicle. And where would they first see one? The evening news.

When Operation Desert Storm began in 1991, the images Americans saw from the battlefield often included a dusty, brown-colored vehicle that seemed to be everywhere. If it wasn't carrying troops, it was storming

down a dusty, desert track with a GI behind a machine gun mounted in back, or fitted with an anti-tank weapon.

Americans came to realize they had a new "jeep," only this time it was called a Humvee and according to GIs it did amazing things. We heard how it could climb a 22-inch vertical wall, rush up a 60 percent grade, and thanks to its all-wheel drive, was almost impossible to get stuck. With independent suspension for both the front and rear wheels, the Humvee could take on all sorts of difficult terrain and never lose traction, and with a ground clearance of 16 inches, it would drive right over almost any obstacle. And though there wasn't much need for water crossings in Desert Storm, the Humvee could ford streams 30 inches deep.

With its all-aluminum body, Humvee are easily transported to the battlefield. As many as 15 can be packed inside a C-5A Galaxy, and the CH-47 Chinook helicopter can haul a pair of Humvees slung underneath.

With all the publicity the Humvee received in Desert Storm, it isn't surprising that in 1992 work was started on a civilian version, which would be nicknamed Hummer. The logical market for a public Hummer would be companies that needed its go-anywhere-anytime abilities, such as utility companies, oil drilling companies, and even search-and-rescue teams.

Eventually, there also were private citizens who took to the Hummer as a reflection of their lifestyle, forming off-road clubs and even holding competitions to see who could take on the roughest of roads. Famed off-road racer

Thanks to its huge driveline, the seat placement in the Hummer H1 puts the driver and three occupants into the far corners of the passenger compartment, where they can barely touch each other. John Lamm

Rod Hall would even build competition Hummers and race them with success.

The biggest surprise, however, was that the Hummer became a darling of the Beverly Hills set from off-road chic to Hummer limousines. Actor Arnold Schwarzenegger was one of the earliest proponents of the "civvie" H1, buying one of the first sold to a private citizen. The second of the actor's very popular Terminator movies had just opened when he got his first Hummer, and he explained to *Road & Track* magazine, "When I drove it for the first time, that's when it became a whole new world. It was not just now so visually interesting for me, but it was perfect when you drive it because the more bumpy the roads got, the smoother the ride got. It doesn't just look ballsy, but it's really rugged in what it can handle. To me, that's the ultimate in a vehicle."

Another of the legendary big, squared-off military-style off-road vehicles was the Lamborghini LM002, which was powered by the Italian automaker's famous V-12 and had a rugged four-wheel drive system. *John Lamm*

Hummer H1s have even been prepared for off-road racing by well-known racer Rod Hall, among others. The H1's ability to withstand a beating and never break comes in handy in the rough world of desert racing. *AM General*

Hummer H1s are featured in any number of movies, probably the most notable is *Broken Arrow* with John Travolta.

The price tag of a civilian Hummer H1 in 2002 was about $110,000, which seems pricey until you realize the number of taxpayer dollars that went into the design and development of the rugged machine and the tens of thousands of Humvees that military services bought to cover that cost. It actually might be one of the great bargains in a vehicle.

There are two body styles: a four-door, four-passenger pickup with an open cargo bed out back and a wagon version that encloses the rear. The earlier two-person model is also still available.

It takes a fairly tall leg to climb up and into a Hummer. Once inside, it's a bit shocking to find so much room allocated to what is basically a four-seater. The seats are separated by a wide, tall center tunnel that contains the hefty drivetrain.

The interior has its share of color coordinating. The instruments have a slightly softer-but-no-nonsense military-spec look to them, though standard equipment includes many of the features found on a car, including air conditioning, power windows, an AM/FM stereo with cassette, and four-wheel anti-lock disc brakes.

The factory option list is fairly short and reflects the H1's original mission and what might be asked of it in civilian life.Those include a trailer towing system, a 12,000-pound winch, cruise control, fuel tank shield, driveline protection, and a high-powered Monsoon sound system with CD changer. Two of the more interesting options are the Central Tire Inflation System that allows the deflation or inflation of the H1's tires while you're driving and—should the tires lose all their air—tires that can run flat for up to 20 miles at 30 mph.

"WHEN I DROVE IT FOR THE FIRST TIME, THAT'S WHEN IT BECAME A WHOLE NEW WORLD."

Arnold Schwarzenegger

Dealer-installed options often take the H1 to a higher level with leather upholstery, high-watt multi-light bars, and sound systems more appropriate for large living rooms.

Civilian H1s aren't lightweights. The open-bed version weighs 6,814 pounds, with the wagon about 350 pounds heavier. To haul that weight around is a 6.5-liter turbocharged General Motors diesel V-8 rated at just 195 horsepower, but developing a whopping 430 foot-pounds of torque developed at only 1,800 rpm. With a four-speed automatic transmission, the speed to 60 mph reads slow at around 18 seconds, but the time does no justice to the feeling of gathering momentum as you accelerate those 3 1/2 tons. There are two ratios in the transfer case and 1.92:1 geared hubs, all the better to help the Hummer literally climb walls. Top speed is just shy of 85 mph.

This is not a subtle machine and you might find yourself humming the Marine Hymn as you rush down the road. Until you get used to it, the 86-1/2-inch width of the H1 leaves you concerned you might sweep a little old lady off a curb on right turns. And nothing short of a loaded gravel truck will intimidate you.

On one of the many Internet Web sites devoted to the Hummer, Jeff Baudin gave some humorous examples of how you know when you are driving an H1, including such tidbits as "annoyances like curbs, speed bumps and fire hydrants are no longer a nuisance," or "your two-car garage has become a one-car garage," and—noting the interior layout—"you can't reach far enough to slap the person sitting in the passenger seat" and "the center console is larger than a Buick trunk."

All in good fun, of course, and part of the urban legend the Hummer H1 has become. And why, General Motors saw fit to lay down its money to buy into that legend and then expand it with the Hummer H2.

AM General's Humvee came to the public's attention during the Gulf War in 1991. It was this awareness that prompted its maker (along with urging by people like actor Arnold Schwarzenegger) to create the civilian H1 Hummer. *AM General*

The Hummer H2's proportions and big wheels are what draw people to it, although the bright yellow paint doesn't hurt. Note the upper window area's lowness compared to the lower body. *John Lamm*

THE JOINING OF GENERALS

THE IDEA FOR GENERAL MOTORS TO SELL A MASS-MARKET CIVILIAN HUMMER INSPIRED AND BUILT BY AM GENERAL IS THE KIND OF DEAL YOU'D THINK WAS COOKED UP IN A SMOKY BACK ROOM.

While hammering out the working relationship required private dinners undoubtedly punctuated by cigar smoke, the impetus for the two Generals to come together came from the public.

By the late 1990s, the sport-utility vehicle market was in full bloom. Customers couldn't seem to get enough of these go-anywhere, do-anything, people-carrying alternatives to the staid minivan. In 1990, just over one million SUVs were sold in America, a number that tripled to over three million by 1999.

Although the bulk of these vehicles were mid-size and full-size trucks, two of the fastest growing segments were the small entry-level versions and large luxury models. All the while, manufacturers were busy conducting market research and looking for the next big thing in SUVs.

Prior to the tie-up with AM General, Kenneth B. Lindensmith, who is now GM's program manager for Hummer, was involved in some of this research. "We saw an emerging segment for a very functional off-road, really tough type of truck," he recalled. "We actually had gone out and developed a concept model and had done some sketches of several proposals."

This proposal, known as Chunk II, was based on a Chevrolet mid-size SUV platform. Designed by Clay Dean, who was brand character chief designer for Chevrolet and GMC, Chunk II was slated to debut at the North American International Auto Show in January 2000.

Long before then, a mockup of the vehicle was used in a Portland, Oregon, marketing clinic.

"Chunk II didn't look like a Hummer, but it had some of those tones," Dean said. "The vehicle was based off the next generation Chevy truck. It was a four-door SUT [sport-utility vehicle with a small pickup bed instead of an enclosed cargo bay]. It was a mid-size vehicle on a 120-inch wheelbase with the wheels pushed out to the corners. It didn't look like a Hummer, but had the same flavor. It had more of an upright windshield and it was definitely not as styled as a traditional car or truck would be. Still, the response in consumer clinics was very positive."

But there was a hitch. "What we found out from that research was that no matter what we did as a brand, if we had the most capable Chevrolet truck on the planet, even better than the Jeep in capability, the response from the public was that they would never give us the credit," Dean said. "We would never be considered as tough. Jeep and Ford were always the top dogs and we were down significantly. Once we threw the Hummer name on the side of the Chunk, we went to the top of the heap."

Internally, GM was undergoing massive change under the direction of Chief Executive Richard Wagoner. His mantra for the new GM was "big and fast," and he was looking for high-profile, fast-track programs as a catalyst for this makeover. Two projects to emerge from this drive were the 2003 Chevy SSR roadster pickup and a new Hummer from GM.

In early 1999, with the results of this research in hand, a small group of GM executives traveled to AM General headquarters outside South Bend, Indiana, and met with its President and CEO Jim Armour to discuss a licensing agreement for the Hummer name to be used on a GM-built SUV.

Armour, an imposing figure with white hair and mustache, is an ex-Ford executive who joined AMC in 1972 and worked with both the Jeep and AM General units, staying with the latter when it was spun off in 1983. Armour guided the company through several ownership changes and the ups-and-downs of defense buildups and budget cutbacks. He studied the way Jeep moved from supplying the military to the mainstream

Leading AM General's management team in the negotiations with General Motors was the company's President and CEO Jim Armour. Armour wanted to make certain the true identity of his company's legendary machine wasn't lost in the shuffle...and it wasn't. *General Motors*

GM designers did an excellent job of reworking the Hummer styling theme for the new GMT-800 platform without losing the square-jawed, rugged feeling of the Humvee-based H1. *John Lamm*

All the rugged feeling of the Hummer H1 comes through in the H2 design with elements like the larger tires—even for SUVs—and the tall front-end approach angle, which is needed for serious off-roading. *Jim Fets/General Motors*

commercial market and felt that there was a similar opportunity for AM General.

"To me, it always seemed obvious that if the Humvee was the latest technology, the best 4x4 in the world, and designed to be the modern replacement for the Jeep, it would eventually go into the commercial arena," Armour explained. "In the 1980s we were busy with a lot of truck programs, and we kept delaying working on the civilian version of the Humvee. In 1988, we talked seriously about it and in 1989 commissioned our engineers to go forward with the project."

In the wake of the success of Desert Storm in 1991, the commercial program began to pick up volume, but this came at the same time as massive defense budget cutbacks. While the company was able to market a couple thousand Hummers a year on the civilian market, drastic cutbacks in government contracts resulted in huge production cuts, which dramatically increased per unit fixed costs. "That more than anything else drove the price up on the H1…just simple absorption of overhead." As a result, loaded civilian Hummers easily topped $100,000.

"Throughout this period, we had talked internally that the next logical step would be a new generation vehicle very much like Jeep and somewhat like Range Rover," Armour recalled. "It would be a new generation vehicle designed specifically for the commercial market with some limited military application. We would actually reverse the roles with the Humvee."

Armour saw two obstacles to this goal; the first was finding the necessary cash. The second was developing the internal expertise to make a vehicle that could compete in the commercial market. "I spent a lot of time trying to figure what it would really take, where we would go to get the people. We would have to go into the marketplace and get a line of credit, roughly $500 million," Armour said. "As I studied this I became more and more convinced that in order to do that, we had to show Wall Street that we had the horses to carry this out. We just

couldn't show them three or four smiling faces and say that's it."

But massive defense cutbacks during the 1990s shelved these plans as AM General fought to preserve its military business. "This whole process focused us internally for five years. We stopped thinking about anything beyond our core military business and what's now called the H1. We just forgot about the next generation Hummer. We were in a fight for our lives." During this period, defense spending dropped by $43 billion. Not only was AM General fighting with other truck makers for a share of the pie, it found itself competing with the large defense contractors who were also looking to save their programs.

"Imagine going to the same committee staffers fighting for funding year after year," Armour said. "By the fifth year they were saying don't come back anymore, you'd better get the Army to fix this problem. We worked with the Army and they fixed the problem, making the funding solid since 1998. At that time, we began getting back to thinking of the commercial market with a new Hummer.

"In late 1998, we began to get soft overtures from various automotive companies," Armour recalled. "We had four or five companies hit us at the same time. We were actually in pretty significant discussions—they weren't really negotiations—when GM called [in 1999]. We had some offshore companies that we were slow-walking, telling them we're kind of busy right now.

"GM did it right from the beginning. Mike DiGiovanni called me requesting a meeting and said they would like to come to us. Some of the other companies asked us to come to them, it's a small thing, but to us it was very significant that the largest automotive company had the manners to say that we want to talk to you about your product, we'd like to visit you. They asked to come with four senior executives. They asked in advance if they could make a presentation.

"Mike explained that they had begun tracking the Hummer as a brand in 1997," Armour said. "They showed us empirical data that confirmed what we knew from less sophisticated means and everything that they said tracked with what we knew already, that the Hummer brand was well established and it is a positive brand and, in particular, it excites young people."

Those initial talks didn't progress very far. "GM came in very focused. They wanted the brand. We told them we don't want to sell the brand. We're in the manufacturing business and we wanted the jobs. We began immediately to sell them on the story that if it makes sense to acquire the Hummer brand because of what it is, it makes even more sense to use the company that created the truck and use the same workforce."

The small band of executives returned to Detroit to reassess their options, including going it alone without the Hummer nameplate on a vehicle styled like the Chunk. About a month later, Ira Rennert, whose Wall Street investment firm purchased AM General in 1992, asked for a follow-up meeting in New York. Paul Schmidt, chief financial officer for GM's North American Operations, attended the meeting in which Rennert again proposed that AM General build an SUV for GM under the Hummer brand.

Schmidt reported back to the Truck Group headed by Tom Davis, who in turn put together a task force headed by Lindensmith to determine if the project was feasible. There were three strengths on which GM hoped to capitalize: AM General's off-road expertise, its manufacturing capability and, most important, the firm's passion for the Hummer product.

While it may seem that AM General was struggling, Lindensmith said the company's manufacturing prowess

> **"I DON'T WANT A LICENSING AGREEMENT FROM AM GENERAL FOR THE NAME, I WANT TO OWN THE NAME, LOCK, STOCK, AND BARREL. IF WE ARE GOING TO DO THIS DEAL, GM HAS TO OWN THE NAME."**
>
> *Tom Davis*

was one of the factors that intrigued him when studying the company as a future partner.

"It's pretty interesting that they were able to take a factory that is capable of building 40,000 units on two shifts and actually make money at 3,000 units a year. We went through the factory and saw some of the innovative things they did to make sure that they could stay afloat even at low volumes."

Lindensmith was also impressed with AM General's plan on how they would add a second model to the line-up and how it could be built in-house. "We felt pretty comfortable with their ability to be set up as an assembler of vehicles," Lindensmith recalls.

But the linchpin in the plan was the product itself.

"We knew we wanted to extend the Hummer portfolio and it wasn't going to be a replacement for the current Hummer," Lindensmith explained. "We needed a vehicle that was a natural extension of the original, but we also needed something that could be built in volume and generate market share. We didn't want to do a little vehicle or even a mid-size vehicle like the Chunk because we felt it wouldn't be true to Hummer at that point in time."

About this time, GM was just launching the new full-size pickup, the GMT-800, and in line were the all-new SUV versions based on this platform. GM was understandably proud of this platform and felt that the next Hummer could be based on this hardware. The AM General people were a bit more skeptical.

"Very early in the discussions, they told us that we have to come clean with the product," GM's Lindensmith recalled. "They told us that if it's just going to be a rebadged Tahoe, they weren't interested in doing a deal with us. They said they'd be perfectly happy to build that kind of vehicle for us, but they wouldn't let us put the Hummer name on it."

Armour says he told GM, "If you're not in it to do a true Hummer, we can't do a deal. It has to do with the passion that is oozing out of everyone here."

Some convincing on both sides was in order. The two companies sent teams to an off-road park outside of Lexington, Kentucky. In addition to the half dozen Hummers brought by AM General, GM had a fleet of GMT-800 products including the as-yet-launched Tahoe/Yukon. It was the diesel-powered, independent suspension Hummers versus the gas-engined, five-link live-axle, full-size SUVs.

"We were very impressed by their vehicles and the places they could go," Lindensmith said. "But also, they were honestly impressed by the mobility of our GMT-800 products. They were particularly impressed with the five-link rear suspension and where we could get off-road with it. But at the end of the day, they took a hose and cleaned off their vehicles and they looked pretty much the way they did when they showed up. We took a hose to our vehicles and we sustained $400, $500, $600 worth of body damage. We got through all the obstacles, it was just rather painful."

During the debriefing that night, Lindensmith described to the AM General team the kind of vehicle they would do based on the Tahoe/Yukon platform. The vehicle would have to have top-notch off-road capability and be able to return to the same trails, go through the exercise and not sustain any body damage. It would have to have a much more passenger-friendly interior than the Hummer in order to attract mainstream buyers. From an on-road perspective, it needed to be easily handled so customers could drive to and from work. But above all, it needed to lead its segment.

"We also talked about diesel versus gas engines," Lindensmith recalled. "We knew the current Hummer lineup was all diesel, but that engine isn't the most important criteria in determining what makes a Hummer. Later in the development process, we tried to package a Duramax diesel in the H2 but found it drove a longer front end and compromised the front approach angle. We said that is not the right thing to do for the vehicle from an off-road perspective, so we stayed with the 6.0-liter gasoline engine only."

Much of what was being discussed at this point in mid-1999 was done based on a memorandum of understanding. No firm deal had been set, and there still were very tricky negotiations to come concerning how this arrangement would work. But already, the GM design staff was hard at work on a clay model that would, by fall 1999, prove instrumental in clinching the deal.

But first, GM had to decide what it wanted from an association with AM General. Very early on, the possibility of acquiring AM General was discussed. That plan was abandoned because it was felt that would destroy a lot of the Hummer character if the company were folded into the larger GM organization. A joint venture also was considered, but dropped because of the many times these arrangements are not clear-cut in terms of who has responsibility for what.

Tom Davis settled on a far different relationship that would prove unique in the auto industry. "I don't want a licensing agreement from AM General for the name," Davis told Lindensmith. "I want to own the name, lock, stock, and barrel. If we are going to do this deal, GM has to own the name." But he also wanted AM General to build the H2 for two reasons: the H2 would be much more credible coming from the company that built the H1 and, with SUV sales so hot, GM didn't have the capacity to build the H2 in the plants producing GMT-800.

Davis also insisted that the deal had to be good for both GM and AM General, that there had to be sufficient incentive on both ends to make a sound business case.

It would take five months to work out the deal. In its simplest terms, AM General sold the Hummer brand

name to General Motors, and in turn, would continue to build the original Hummer—now called the H1—under license to be sold through a new dealer network established by GM. Of the 55 Hummer dealers that existed before the deal, nearly half were already GM dealers. The balance were either bought out or converted to GM franchises. AM General would retain the rights to build and sell the Humvee for military applications, free of any licensing fees. But more important, AM General would be the contract builder of 40,000 Hummer H2s per year in a new plant in Mishawaka, Indiana, built by GM for AM General.

Until October 1999, the final contract language continued to be negotiated. The question of what the actual vehicle would look like was still unanswered. Armour had a vision for the vehicle in his mind and GM company executives didn't know what Armour was thinking and naturally were apprehensive about his approach.

It was during these intricate negotiations that Lindensmith suggested to Armour that they take a break and visit GM's advanced design studio to see a clay model of the H2 concept. GM hoped to unveil the show vehicle at the Detroit show in January 2000 as a way of announcing the deal with AM General.

"Jim's kind of a quiet guy," Lindensmith said. "He walked around and around and wasn't saying anything. I thought he either really loves this thing or hates this thing—I wasn't sure which."

Armour recalled walking around the vehicle, taking it all in, not saying much because in his mind it was a Hummer. He just assumed that everyone was on the same page and he didn't realize how anxious the GM side was to get his feedback. When Lindensmith asked him what he thought, Armour replied, "You got it. You guys understand exactly what this thing wants to be."

At that point, Lindensmith breathed a huge sigh of relief. He knew he had a deal. Despite all the negotiation left to go on this extremely complicated contract, GM was going to make the Hummer H2 a reality.

On Dec. 21, 1999, GM and AM General announced that GM had acquired exclusive ownership of the Hummer name worldwide and that the two companies would pursue product, marketing and distribution opportunities.

It was during the North American International Auto Show, however, on Jan. 11, when the H2 show vehicle was presented that the full extent and ambitious scope of the agreement was revealed.

Ron Zarrella, who was then president of the GM's North American Operations, said, "The Hummer H2 vision vehicle provides a look at what the future of Hummer could be and demonstrates how GM plans to uphold a tradition based on aggressiveness and toughness while strategically growing the brand." But more important was the following promise: "Speed to market is a priority for General Motors. Production of the first jointly developed product will begin in the 2002 calendar year."

The ink had barely dried on the contract and GM was promising to jointly develop an all-new vehicle created by a team of engineers that had barely been formed, and to assemble that vehicle in a yet-to-be-built factory—all in two year's time. This in an industry that considers 36 months fast for a complete redesign of an existing vehicle built in an existing plant.

"The need to get to market quickly was an overriding concern," Armour explained. "You've got to hit the market now; the longer the wait, the less accuracy you have. GM was looking for a program that needed to go fast and this was it."

Not only was GM promising a new Hummer, it promised to deliver it to market in record time.

General Motors based the Hummer H2 on its GMT-800 chassis, which was developed for its first new light trucks of the 21st century, like this Chevrolet Tahoe. *General Motors*

The look of a vehicle's "face" is crucial to its overall design. GM designers sketched several ideas for the grille, headlights, and protective bars for the front of the H2. *General Motors*

A NEW KIND OF HUMMER

IN JUNE 1999, CLAY DEAN HAD RECENTLY FINISHED THE CHUNK II CONCEPT VEHICLE FOR THE 2000 NORTH AMERICAN INTERNATIONAL AUTO SHOW WHEN WAYNE CHERRY, GM'S VICE PRESIDENT OF DESIGN, CALLED HIM INTO HIS OFFICE.

"Something is going on here," he told Dean. "Essentially, GM may acquire the Hummer name and what I want you to do on your own is start drawing some potential new Hummers that we could do as a concept vehicle. We're going to cancel the concept you've done and we're going to do an all-new one."

But Cherry wasn't finished. "Don't talk to any of your guys," he cautioned, "don't tell anyone in the studio; sketch it at home, after work."

Dean had to create an all-new Hummer that would satisfy the broad goals set forth in the negotiations between GM and AM General. Except Dean was not privy to the negotiations.

Dean spent a good portion of that early summer studying the original Hummer and sketching potential Hummers into all hours of the night.

"At that point, I hadn't been given a package, it was more trying to get a flavor and feel for it," Dean explained. "Everyone knows what a Hummer is. Visually, this new vehicle had to be completely understandable as Hummer. We weren't trying to replace the H1, we were trying to extend the brand. We were trying to add to something that is well established. The only thing we could do to the Hummer is screw it up."

Dean said the starting point was to understand why the Hummer looks the way it does. "It is very sheer; the wheels are at the corners, the body side doesn't have tumble home [the way a car curves inward from the base of the windshield and side glass to the roof]. It's very upright, like a prefabricated shed, which is what endears it to people. It is so cool and it is so different than anything else."

Function drove the original Hummer design. The wheels are out at the corners to provide steep approach and departure angles for off-road ability. The slab sides

Finished at the last minute for display at the 2000 Detroit Auto Show was the design prototype. GM remained very faithful to the prototype when building the production H2, though the two share no body panels.
John Lamm

are an efficient way to package the mechanicals and the upright front windshield is angled that way to minimize the vehicle's radar signature.

"We wanted to take that same basic feel and philosophy —the wheels at the corners, the upper glass area that is very thin, very bunker-like—but we also wanted to throw in a degree of contemporary style, a more integrated look that would be a new direction," Dean said.

By August word was out about the talks between AM General and GM, so Dean was able to take his sketches

The Hummer H2 after its unveiling at the 2002 Los Angeles Auto Show, just two short years after the prototype was shown. None of the aura of the concept vehicle was lost when the design was produced. *John Lamm*

to his team and begin working in earnest on the H2 concept vehicle that would debut in less than six months at the Detroit show.

At that time, word was leaking out that GM was working on a Baby Hummer. "It wasn't much of a baby," Dean laughed, pointing out that in some regards the H2 is actually taller and longer than the H1.

In capturing the Hummer's essence in the new design, Dean relied on some key words and phrases as inspiration. "The words we started with were *defiant, overbuilt, in-your-face, very aggressive, militaristic*," Dean recalled. "The longer we talked about it, though, we polished up the words so they weren't as raw. The key words became *intimidating, unstoppable, capable, exclusive, no compromise.*

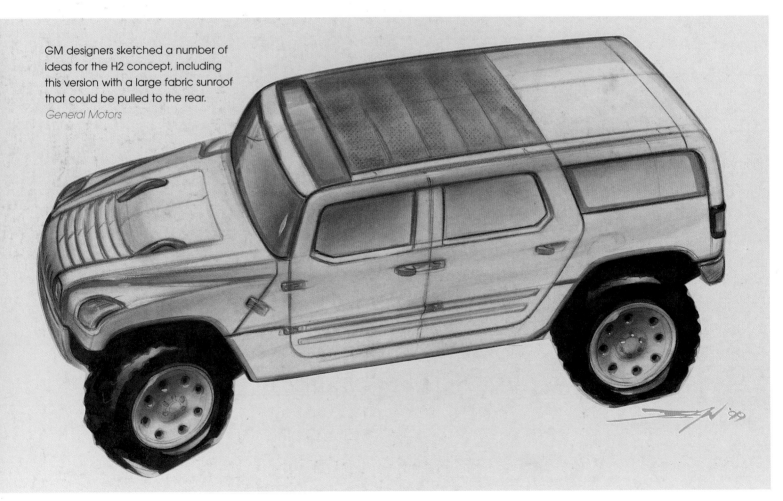

GM designers sketched a number of ideas for the H2 concept, including this version with a large fabric sunroof that could be pulled to the rear.
General Motors

Among the ideas sketched for the Hummer H2 was the fastback version that mimics one of the many versions of the H1 that AM General builds for the military.
General Motors

We felt that Hummer starts where everybody else's road ends. That's what we wanted the vehicle to convey."

While trying to capture this essence, Dean was also acutely aware of being able to address some of the deficiencies of the original. "We had to find those areas that people don't like about the Hummer," Dean said. "Not being able to carry enough people was one of them. Having an interior that has a feeling of more spaciousness was another. We wanted to appeal to people who want to live this Hummer lifestyle, bucking the mainstream, not being a conformist, not wanting to be an everyday SUV drone."

Above all, the designers wanted a package that worked well and was easier to live with on a daily basis. This refinement in both function and appearance was a critical element in the overall approach.

"When you look at industrial goods like supercomputers or things of that nature, there is a cleanliness, a sheerness, and a purposefulness that is all there," Dean explained. "Where the original Hummer was raw and rugged, we wanted to make the H2 refined and tough. A lot of the elements of the concept vehicle have transitioned to the production vehicle. You can see that attention to detail where one line joining two elements of the design would have been five or six lines on the H1. For instance, we have one line separating the door, windshield, and hood panel, while on the H1, there's a line dividing the door, a flange panel with another line, a second flange, then the windshield."

Dean points out that the basic shape of the vehicle is very simple, pure, and straightforward. All the windows, except for the door glass, are flush mounted, adding to the clean look. Unlike the original, which uses riveted aluminum body panels, the H2 has a steel body. "One thing we took a little heat on from the purists was the lack of rivets," Dean admitted, adding that he prefers the smoother, more modern look of the steel body panels.

Originally, Dean had planned to put the H2 concept on a 130-inch wheelbase, but ended up with just under a 123-inch wheelbase, which is closer in dimension to the GMT-800 upon which the production vehicle would be built. Dean said the longer wheelbase is necessary to create the cradle effect of the door apertures. "You couldn't get that effect on the Tahoe's short wheelbase, so we ended up creating a unique wheelbase for the H2," he said, pointing out that the actual production version of the H2 grew from the original 116-inch wheelbase of the Tahoe to 122.8 inches.

One design element from the H1 that Dean made an integral part of the H2 is the shape of the doors. The original Hummer was never designed to have roll-down windows. When AM General added them to the Hummer, they had to go outboard to mount the window mechanisms. As a result, the doors are popped out on the H1. "As a car designer, that's not something you do on purpose," Dean observed. "But it became such an icon of what the vehicle was, we decided we needed to do pop-out doors to have this feel. It's one of those simple

> ## "WE NEVER DEBATED THE FACE OF THE VEHICLE, IT WOULD HAVE TO HAVE SEVEN SLOTS IN A LINEAR ENVIRONMENT."
>
> *Clay Dean*

cues so that if you put the two vehicles side-by-side you pick up on it right away."

That the H2 would be instantly recognizable as a Hummer was the overriding concern of the designers. "We did a clinic in California and had a bunch of pictures of the scale models along with an H1. None was branded and people said the H2 is a Hummer," Dean said. Just to be sure, GM management commissioned two other Hummer models, one from its California design team and another at GM Design Staff in Warren, Michigan. Both were immediately rejected in favor of the H2.

"If there was one goal of the vehicle, it was that it had to be unmistakably Hummer. People have to be 200 yards down the road and recognize it as one," Dean emphasized.

When you put the H1 and H2 side-by-side, they appear quite different yet have the same composition. That composition is in the details, from the upright windshield, to the air boxes between the firewall and fenders, to the hood that tilts forward. Even the face is the same, with the seven-slot grille inboard-mounted headlamps and integrated brush guard.

"We never debated the face of the vehicle, it would have to have seven slots in a linear environment," Dean said. "I don't think anyone in their right mind would confuse this with Jeep because of the sheer bulk and proportion of the vehicle."

DaimlerChrysler, which owns the Jeep brand, sued GM and sought an injunction to halt production of the H2 because it used a seven-slot grille. DaimlerChrysler contended that this arrangement was unique to Jeep, even though the original Hummer also had a seven-slot grille. The judge in the case ruled against the injunction and in GM's favor, thus allowing production to go forward.

Hummers should be aggressive. Here you can see one designer's imagination as he sketched the mood of the machine
with a row of spotlights, a mean stance, and a rock-killing skid plate. *General Motors*

"The look we have is unique to Hummer, but we wanted to evolve it further," Dean explained. The inboard-mounted headlamps, which are flanked by outboard-mounted turn signals, are encased in brightwork with seven slots. Below the grille, there's a bumper/brush-guard/skid plate combination that replaces the traditional lower fascia found on most vehicles.

Another interesting facet of the H2 design is its overall proportion. It is wide and tall, yet the body looks low because most of the height comes from the large, 35-inch-tall wheels that offer tremendous ground clearance.

In addition to impressing AM General's Jim Armour with the clay mockup, the designers also impressed Hummer's number one customer, Arnold Schwarzenegger. He was given a sneak peek of the vehicle in November 1999 and, in fact, the company code-name for the H2 was Project Maria (named for Schwarzenegger's wife, Maria Schriver).

"So this is Maria, the beast," Schwarzenegger said when looking at the mockup. He liked what he saw, making a few suggestions, such as giving the vehicle a third-row seat and thicker A-pillars to give the H2 a stronger presence.

A modeler in the GM studios puts finishing touches on the grille of the H2's clay model as the design was being developed. *General Motors*

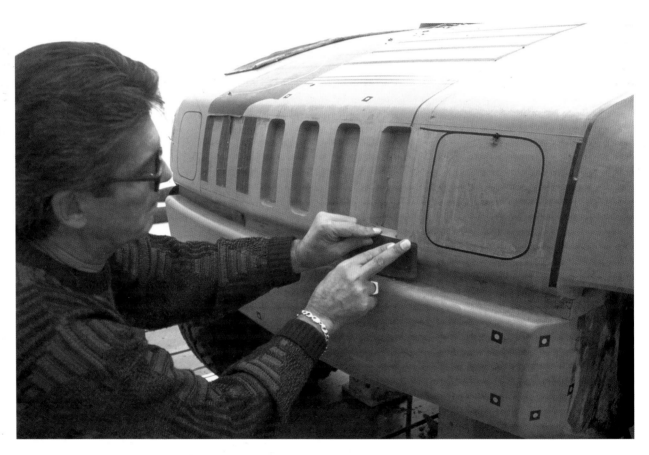

After the basic design of the Hummer H2 was approved, a full-scale model was created in clay so designers and executives could see how the shape would look. *General Motors*

Pleasing the AM General people and potential customers like Schwarzenegger is one thing, getting the H2 ready for the auto show was entirely different, and almost didn't happen.

"We did the vehicle over at Venture Industries, a nearby supplier," Dean recalled. "For four months we moved over there, all our designers, all our sculptors. We took over two rooms and had a full-on Hummer studio there. The press kit photos were shot in our studios—we moved the vehicle out and draped paint cloths all over the room. It had no interior, we taped on the mirrors and

two bolts were holding on the grille. All these headlamp lenses were stuck on with double-sided tape.

"It was a nightmare; we lived in that studio for four days straight, in 24-hour shifts, to keep it going. At about 5 A.M. the day of the 1 P.M. press introduction, I was sitting there looking at the vehicle...there was no glass in it, it didn't run, the seats weren't in, the inner fenders weren't in, and the wheels weren't bolted on."

Dean said workers were literally assembling the concept in the semi on the way down to Detroit's Cobo Hall. Finally, it made it into the hall, but while it was being driven up the ramp to the back of the stage, it shorted out and quit. It was choreographed that the vehicle would be driven out after Zarrella made the announcement about the agreement with AM General.

"The engine wouldn't start, the battery was dead, but it worked out pretty cool because it was pushed onto the stage where it rolled out silently," said Dean, who was riding in the passenger seat. "No one knew what was coming."

Dean was to give a little speech that he hastily put together before the press conference. "Unbeknownst to me, the seats weren't bolted in, so when I went to get out, I was almost thrown out of the vehicle. But it was there. Every day for the next three days, the show car team was there, bolting everything together. By the end of the show it was actually all together."

While the production H2 is fairly faithful to the concept in appearance, there isn't a single body panel shared by the two vehicles. Another big difference is the interior. On the show truck, Dean wasn't constrained by the GMT-800 interior architecture.

"The one area we felt was really weak on the Hummer H1 was the interior," Dean said. "For as exciting as the exterior was, the interior was a complete letdown. One of the things we wanted to do on the interior of this concept was to have a sense of drama. We wanted to have a big canvas top. We wanted to have a lot of gauges. We wanted it to be a command center. We wanted leathers, hammer-toned metals, anodized aluminum, billet aluminum."

The H2 concept has a unique look and feel with instruments clustered over the top of the steering column, encased in billet aluminum bezels. A large center console is equipped with a shifter that resembles the throttle lever

> "AT ABOUT 5 A.M. THE DAY OF THE 1 P.M. PRESS INTRODUCTION, THERE WAS NO GLASS IN IT, IT DIDN'T RUN, THE SEATS WEREN'T IN, THE INNER FENDERS WEREN'T IN, AND THE WHEELS WEREN'T BOLTED ON."
>
> *Clay Dean*

of a jetliner. Additional instrumentation, such as an inclinometer and altimeter, adorn the dash's center stack. It's a high tech, luxurious environment thanks to the extensive use of leather and aluminum accents.

As for the leather, Dean revealed a little secret. When the hides for the interior were delivered just before the Christmas holiday, it was discovered that they didn't quite match the color of the rest of the interior. With no ability to have the hides redone, Dean suggested that they be flipped over and used as contrasting suede.

The other major difference between the show and production trucks is the decision to use regular production door handles from the GMT-800, getting rid of the exposed chromed hinges and dropping the taillamps out of the C-pillar to a more conventional location on either side of the tailgate.

Dean didn't follow the H2 into production. Instead, he handed the program off to veteran designer Terry Henline, who not only had to reconcile the H2 concept within the constricts of the GMT-800 package provided by the development team, but produce a second show truck for the 2001 New York Auto Show.

This model would be an SUT, like Dean's original sketches. At first, it was thought they'd use the tooling for the H2 concept and make a pickup out of it. But already, the program was moving so fast toward the production truck, it was decided to base the second concept off production sheet metal.

"If you park the H2 and H2 SUT next to each other, you can see the progression," Dean said. "But separate them and they look the same. It's neat how close we kept to the vision. It's really a testament to Terry Henline and his team that they didn't try to redesign the whole vehicle. There wasn't time and they knew it was good enough to begin with."

"Extreme functionality was the overriding objective in designing the H2 SUT concept," Henline said. As a result, the chromed body jewelry, including the exposed hinges, was eliminated, although the external hood latch was retained as an important visual cue. Blacked-out

bumpers with integrated tow hooks and receiver hitches front and rear replaced the front and rear skid plates. The polished chrome grille was retained, along with hood hooks used to tilt the deck forward.

But the most important aspect was that the H2 SUT used production body panel surfaces, a modified GMT-800 drivetrain, chassis, and interior architecture. While the original H2 concept sported an independent rear suspension, the H2 SUT and the production H2 utilize a five-link live-axle setup.

Inside, the SUT has a more conventional steering wheel, with built-in controls, a traditional instrument cluster recessed into the dash and a center stack that houses the sound system and climate controls. The shifter was toned down a bit, though it still retains the jet throttle look; large circular vents reinforce the aircraft cockpit feel. Other items found on the show truck included 360-degree infrared night vision, a GPS satellite navigation system, and several 110-volt power outlets.

The SUT also sports a rear bulkhead that has a power-retractable window. With the window down, the bulkhead can be folded forward to enlarge the cargo bed.

With the strong visual link established between the H2 and H1, Dean said the designers are now freed up a bit to take future Hummers a bit further. "This design can run for 10 years. In a way, it's like the Beetle, you don't have to do a lot to it," Dean said. Along the way, however, look for different interior packages, more use of carbon fiber, maybe a special ops version inspired by the military. "Still, we are in a planting and harvesting strategy with the design. We've planted the seed of a contemporary Hummer with the H2 and now we can harvest from the next generation of vehicle. The next Hummer can be much more progressive than the H2 and move even further from the H1."

Looking back on the process that led to the design of the H2, Dean believes that though pressures to get the design right and get it down quickly were tremendous, on a philosophical level, it was easier to remake an icon than starting from scratch.

"It was like doing a Corvette," Dean said, recalling his earlier work on the C5. "Sure there are a lot of experts coming out of the woodwork who know what

The exterior of the Hummer H2 concept didn't change much when done for production, but the interior did—as can be seen when comparing this photo of the show car's dash with those of H2s now headed for dealerships. *John Lamm* the next Corvette or Hummer should look like, but on the other hand, everyone understands what you are doing. Everyone knows what a Corvette is, you can look through hundreds of sketches and say that's Corvette, or that's not Corvette. But if someone said to me, design a two-seat Chevrolet sports car, well, what do you want it to be? You want it to be cute? You want it to be masculine? You want it to be feminine? Do you want it to be graceful, nostalgic, contemporary or futuristic?

"That is where we were with the Chunk II. Design an aggressive, outdoor, militaristic-type vehicle. What is it? Is contemporary? Is it retro? Is it funky? With a Hummer you know exactly what you are doing. It's very easy to tailor up or down how contemporary it's going

It was a rush to get the Hummer H2 concept vehicle ready for the 2000 Detroit Auto Show. After the craziness and the show were over, the design team had a chance to finally pose with their baby. *General Motors*

A classic General Motors photo: The Hummer H2 concept vehicle photographed outside the styling dome at the automaker's huge design center, taking the same pose as generations of GM machines, from Cadillac sedans to Corvettes. *General Motors*

to be. You put sketches on the wall that have some Hummer cues, but it might be too cute. You can edit things very fast.

"SUVs have become such a commodity," Dean continued. "They are modern-day minivans and station wagons. They have great function. You can line them all up from Ford to GM to Toyota and each one will have some unique features, but from 200 yards away can you look and say, "What's so different about them?" The one that stands out the most is the H2. Here is a vehicle that functions every bit as well as the others and yet it's an individual. It makes a strong statement that I'm not like you guys. I'm unique. I have personality and this is what I stand for."

General Motors modified the mechanical pieces of its new GMT-800 chassis for the Hummer H2. Among other things, GM made certain all underbody components were flush with the bottom of the frame rails to prevent their damage in off-roading. *Jim Fets/General Motors*

CHAPTER 4

GIVING H2 BACKBONE

THE IDEA TO UTILIZE THE GMT-800 ARCHITECTURE MIGHT BE VIEWED AS A MASTERSTROKE IN GETTING H2 TO MARKET IN RECORD TIME. WHILE IT'S TRUE THERE IS SOME SYNERGY IN PARTS SHARING AND DEVELOPMENT TIME, THE TEAM UNDER THE DIRECTION OF PROGRAM MANAGER KENNETH LINDENSMITH MADE SOME SIGNIFICANT CHANGES THAT ENSURED THE FINISHED PRODUCT HAD A CHARACTER IN KEEPING WITH THE HUMMER LEGEND.

"Our intent was to pull about 50 percent of our production parts off the GMT-800," Lindensmith explained. "In reality, we're sitting at about 40 percent. Every time we made a decision on making a change, we did it because it was right for the vehicle."

Lindensmith's team was formed in October 1999, aided by an outside engineering firm from Germany by the name of EDAG. Lindensmith also picked up several engineers from AM General.

The first step was to evaluate the GMT-800 platform and determine what could and could not be used.

"We knew we needed short overhangs for good approach and departure angles, as well as good ground clearance," Lindensmith said. "We also knew that this vehicle would be pretty heavy. The five-link suspension was only available in a half-ton variety, so we knew we had to upgrade the rear suspension to be able to do that. We knew we wanted to put the biggest tires we could find on this thing because that adds a lot to the vehicle's off-road mobility."

The ability to have serious off-road capability was a major driving force behind the design and modification of the GMT-800 mechanicals. All components needed to be mounted or packaged flush with or above the bottom of the frame rails in order to ensure that critical components would be protected from underbody impacts. This flush surface combined with rocker panel protection also enables the H2 to slide over obstacles. Finally, with no low-hanging parts, the vehicle is less likely to get caught on projections like tree stumps.

A complete Hummer chassis shows the packaging required to fit the torsion bar front suspension, the five-link rear suspension, the exhaust system, and the sort of perimeter protection provided for serious off-roading.
General Motors

The H2 has an exceptionally long wheelbase when compared to its overall length. It rides on a 122.8-inch. wheelbase compared to its overall length of 189.8 inches. With short overhangs front and rear, the coil-spring version of the H2 has a 40.4-degree approach angle and a 39.6-degree departure angle when fitted with LT315/70R17 tires. A lower profile tire was initially going to be offered, which reduced these angles, but it was decided to go with the taller tires as standard equipment. H2 models with air suspension have an approach angle of 41.7 degrees and a departure angle of 38.1 degrees. The ramp brakeover angles are a respective 25.8 and 25.6 degrees for the coil and air suspension. The minimum ground clearance is 10 inches for the coil spring setup and 10 1/2 inches with the air suspension. On both models, the axle differential-to-ground clearance is 9.9 inches.

Underpinning the H2 is a fully welded, ladder-type frame. It is comprised of three modules and is fully boxed, with hydro-formed front and rear modules, to provide exceptional rigidity. In addition, special attention was paid to the front and rear modules with added reinforcements to control the frame's ability to absorb energy and to crush and collapse in a collision.

Again, the frame's cross members around the transmission mounting points are made as flat as possible to eliminate protrusions that could cause the vehicle to get hung up on obstacles. Attachment points for the drivetrain have been optimized to reduce the potential for vibrations to be transmitted to the passenger cabin.

"If you look at the frame, our plan was to use the front end of a 3/4-ton truck and the rear end of the 1/2-ton truck and just meld them together," Lindensmith said.

> **"IF YOU LOOK AT THE FRAME, OUR PLAN WAS TO USE THE FRONT END OF A 3/4-TON TRUCK AND THE REAR END OF THE 1/2-TON TRUCK AND JUST MELD THEM TOGETHER."**
>
> *Kenneth Lindensmith*

"But if you go look to the changes we have made to the frame to beef it up and make it the way it has to be, it is still the same design concept, but they aren't the same parts anymore. We would categorize it as a modified part that we're using."

One of the modifications to the front frame section, in addition to its beefier construction, is GM's first standard winch receiver, which is designed to accommodate a 9,000-pound winch unit. Extensions to the winch receiver have been designed to allow for the use of optional bike racks and other carriers. This receiver is the same as the one used on the rear for the trailer hitch. The mount for this receiver is built right into the front cross member, which is also the attaching point for dual front tow hooks.

Using a stamped-steel box section, the mid-frame carries the bulk of the passenger cabin and is the mounting point for the transmission and transfer case. It is formed to provide mounting space for the composite 33-gallon fuel tank on the left inside frame rail just ahead of the rear axle.

The rear-frame module kicks up dramatically to provide the high departure angle and is heavily reinforced to provide a solid base for the H2's 8,600-pound GVWR capacity. Like the front winch receiver, the plug-in for the trailer hitch is built right into the last cross member of the frame and the H2 is equipped with a Class III trailer hitch as standard equipment.

There is additional underbody protection in the form of large skid plates and rocker guards. A 4.0-mm stamped aluminum cover extends from the bottom of the front bumper back underneath the vehicle to the firewall. The H2 logo is stamped into the front portion of this piece and is visible when looking head-on at the vehicle.

A small, ladder-type shield made of 1 inch tubes is bolted behind this piece to protect the transmission and catalytic converters, and has the strength to support the entire weight of the vehicle if it becomes high-centered. A smaller shield made of galvanized sheet steel protects the transfer case. This piece is bowed to spring back into its original shape if it strikes a rock. An additional composite shield that offers protection from abrasions and punctures also shrouds the fuel tank.

Beneath the rocker panels are black steel tubes bolted directly to the frame. These run along the vehicle sides, protecting the door sills and lower door panels from damage. These bars are strong enough to support the entire weight of the vehicle.

The entire frame is carefully mounted to the H2's body by a three-point mounting system that isolates the front module to reduce the transmission of engine noise and vibration into the cabin. The axle is connected to the frame by two vertical forward mounts; the rear mount is attached directly to a frame cross member that fits between the lower control arm brackets.

That front suspension is a torsion bar setup with 46-mm monotube gas-charged shocks and a 35.9-mm tubular front stabilizer bar. The front axle can carry 4,000 pounds. The dampers—specifically designed for off-road use—have a large, 40-mm center tube.

The suspension also has a two-stage bump stop feature that allows it to handle two different levels of sudden impacts. Primary jounce bumpers, like on any vehicle, protect the frame from being hit by the suspension on severe impacts. Secondary bumpers which are integrated into the shocks, slow the suspension travel before it hits

THE ENTIRE FRAME IS CAREFULLY MOUNTED TO THE H2'S BODY BY A THREE-POINT MOUNTING SYSTEM THAT ISOLATES THE FRONT MODULE TO REDUCE THE TRANSMISSION OF ENGINE NOISE AND VIBRATION INTO THE CABIN.

the primary bump stop to reduce the severity of the jolt to the cabin. This design was adapted from high-speed desert racing vehicles and provides excellent ride control on bumpy roads.

The H2 has a choice of two rear suspensions: the standard, coil spring, five-link trailing arm setup or an optional self-leveling air spring suspension, which is part of the off-road package and includes an air compressor and tire inflation system.

The standard five-link suspension uses stamped-steel lower control arms and forged steel upper arms; the rear end is located by a track bar. The coil springs have variable rates and long shock absorbers for good suspension travel in an off-road environment. The coil springs' variable rate is tuned for two comfort levels: a softer rate for on-road use and a progressively stiffer rate that increases in proportion to the force of the spring input. In other words, if you're traveling over an undulating or rough surface, the spring rate actually increases in proportion to the speed and force with which the spring is compressed. Likewise, in cornering, as the springs load with the centrifugal force of the body, they progressively stiffen and reduce the amount of vehicle roll. Helping to provide additional lateral stability is a 30-mm rear stabilizer bar.

The self-leveling air suspension includes a high-capacity compressor that offers an even longer suspension stroke than the coil-spring suspension, for increased off-road capability. The shocks likewise have a longer travel and a larger diameter rod for more durability.

In addition to providing greater suspension articulation, the air suspension offers the benefit of automatic load leveling and the ability to select the ride height of

Each Hummer's rugged body has been designed for high structural rigidity, which not only adds to its off-road abilities but also virtually eliminates squeaks and rattles during normal driving. *General Motors*

An example of the detailing on the new Hummer: its name, H2, is emblazoned on the 4-mm stamped-aluminum skid plate, which extends from the bottom of the bumper back underneath the vehicle to the firewall. *Jim Fets/General Motors*

the rear end. As the vehicle is loaded, sensors detect any drop in ride height and automatically pump more air into the springs to bring the vehicle back into a level attitude. These sensors are attached directly to the suspension links, which monitor any deviation from standard height. The compressor is equipped with an air dryer to remove moisture from the compressed air that might degrade the springs.

IF YOU'RE TRAVELING OVER AN UNDULATING OR ROUGH SURFACE, THE SPRING RATE ACTUALLY INCREASES IN PROPORTION TO THE SPEED AND FORCE WITH WHICH THE SPRING IS COMPRESSED.

The driver is also able to manually select an extended ride height mode that will raise the rear end to improve the departure angle. When the vehicle's transfer case is in 4 LO, a ride height switch increases air pressure in the springs lifting the rear end by two inches to increase the departure angle to 41.8 degrees, the ramp break-over angle to 27 1/2 degrees, and boosts minimum running ground clearance to 10.8 inches. This feature allows the H2 to literally lift itself off obstacles if it becomes hung up.

Once the vehicle attains a speed of 20 miles per hour or higher, the system automatically lets air out of the springs to return the vehicle to its normal ride height. At speeds above 50 miles per hour, it will slightly lower the rear end to improve stability.

The Hummer H2 rides on LT315/70R17 all-terrain tires on both the standard and off-road-package

This set of dashboard-mounted switches control the tow/haul mode, engage the secondary traction control mode, and, on H2s with air suspension, includes a button to extend ride height. *John Lamm*

equipped models. The off-road package features rim protection, a reinforcement of the tire over the rim and
helps keep the tire locked in place when the tire pressure
is reduced for additional traction on sand and loose dirt.
These tires also feature triple sidewalls to reduce the
chance of punctures.

The brakes on the H2 are four-wheel discs with dual
piston calipers, four-channel ABS, and Dynamic Rear
Proportioning. This latter feature constantly monitors
wheel speed and automatically modulates fore-and-aft
brake pressure to make
sure that the braking
loads are evenly distrib-
uted over the two axles. It
not only reduces wear on
the front brakes, but also
provides better weight distribution and increased
braking efficiency. A
hydraulic booster pro-
vides the assist to the
power brakes.

Brake tuning on a vehi-
cle with multiple uses like
the H2 is no simple task.
The ABS has been adjust-
ed to accommodate oper-
ation over a wide range of
surfaces. For instance, on
gravel roads a bit of slip
has been programmed
into the system to prevent
the wheels from locking
up or aggressively engag-

**AS THE VEHICLE
IS LOADED, SEN-
SORS DETECT
ANY DROP IN
RIDE HEIGHT AND
AUTOMATICALLY
PUMP MORE AIR
INTO THE
SPRINGS TO
BRING THE VEHI-
CLE BACK INTO A
LEVEL ATTITUDE.**

ing the ABS system. This slip allows the wheels to dig in a
little deeper rather than skate over the surface and actually
helps to slow the vehicle quicker. Also, the system is programmed to identify pothole impacts and prevent the ABS
from cycling.

With both the steel and air spring suspensions, Hummers
ride on LT315/70R17 all-terrain tires with rim protection
that allows tire pressure to be dropped for better traction
on sand and loose dirt without danger of deflation.
John Lamm

An H2's go-anywhere, do-anything abilities are aided by the fact that the driveline has three transfer-case settings, two rear differential selections, and two traction control options, yielding up to seven different driving modes. *Jim Fets/General Motors*

Good front approach and rear departure angles are important for an off-road machine. The H2s have a generous 40.4 degrees approach and 39.6 degrees departure when the vehicle is fitted with the coil spring suspension.
Jim Fets/General Motors

The H2 uses the ABS system as a platform for traction control. This traction aid works entirely through the vehicle's braking system and doesn't rely on reducing engine torque to regain grip.

The traction control system is interfaced with the vehicle's transfer case to determine the level of intervention and whether the rear axle differential lock should be engaged.

This advanced approach to traction allows the system to detect slip in a single wheel and automatically apply the brake to slow it down and transfer torque across the differential to the wheel that has more traction. This allows the H2 to have three wheels on a slippery surface and use the one wheel with grip to move the vehicle forward, even on a 10 percent grade.

The single-wheel approach can induce yaw; however, the system is calibrated to apply brake pressure gently and gradually when the transfer case is in the high range. If the low range is selected, the brake intervention is more aggressive, giving the quicker response needed in an off-road situation where one wheel may be barely touching the ground. In that case, if the system doesn't respond instantly, the lightly loaded tire could quickly start spinning.

The traction control system has an additional program called TC2 for use whenever the center or rear differentials are in a locked mode. When the TC2 button is engaged, it allows additional wheel slip, which can keep the vehicle moving on loose soil or sand. This additional mode allows the driver to specifically match the drivetrain action to the surface the vehicle is traveling over, including paved roads, snow, ice, deep mud, gravel, sand, or rock climbing.

With three transfer-case settings, two rear differential selections, and two traction control options, the H2 offers up to seven different driving modes. With such a wide range of drivetrain options, the engineers knew they had to have an engine that could deliver the goods. They found the right one in GM's parts bin.

While the Hummer H1 has a 6.5-liter turbodiesel V-8, GM opted for a non-turbo 6.0-liter gasoline engine for the H2, using its Vortec 6000 V-8 for its ability to motivate the SUV both on- and off-road. *Jim Fets/General Motors*

CHAPTER 5

MIGHT MAKES RIGHT

FROM A DESIGN PERSPECTIVE, THE HUMMER H2 HAS CAPTURED THE ESSENCE OF THE ORIGINAL H1 WHILE USING A MODERN APPROACH TO ITS EXECUTION. THE SHAPE OF THE STEEL-BODIED H2 IS MORE REFINED THAN THE RIVETED ALUMINUM SHELL OF THE H1, YET THERE'S NO MISTAKING THE LINEAGE.

It's the same story with the chassis—the original boasts a fully independent suspension while the H2 uses an innovative five-link rear end that gives the newer version almost the same level of off-road capability.

Beneath the hood, the two Hummers are quite different: The H1 uses a turbodiesel and the H2 employs a normally aspirated 6.0-liter gasoline V-8. The decision to go this route was so the H2 would deliver the kind of performance expected from a vehicle that competes not only with rugged off-roaders, but also with the new class of luxury SUVs that rarely leave the highway.

To understand the difference, you first have to consider why a turbodiesel was selected for the original Hummer. This 6.5-liter V-8 produces what seems to be a meager 195 brake horsepower at 3,400 rpm. The real value of the diesel, though, is its prodigious torque, which is rated at 430 foot-pounds at just 1,800 rpm. This gives the H1 the ability to crawl out of mud holes, up steep inclines, and over rocky terrain with the greatest of ease. Because the diesel uses compression ignition technology, there's little in the way of engine electrics to get

Matched to the V-8 and its heavy-duty four-speed automatic transmission is a Borg-Warner two-speed electronically controlled transfer case, which offers High and Lo ranges and can be used open or locked.
General Motors

wet or to fail in the field. Diesels are rugged, durable, and fairly easy to maintain; huge advantages in military service.

The downside of the turbodiesel is the noise, smoky exhaust, and limited top speed, attributes that are tolerable off-road, but difficult to live with in an urban or suburban environment. As a result, the H2 team decided that a powerful gasoline V-8 was the way to go. In GM's vast powertrain inventory, the perfect candidate was found in the 6.0-liter Vortec 6000 V-8. This normally aspirated, overhead valve (OHV) V-8 makes 316 brake horsepower at 5,200 rpm and 360 foot-pounds of

General Motor's highly regarded Vortec 6000 pushrod V-8 produces 316 brake horsepower at 5,200 rpm and—important for rugged off-road trails—a strong 360 foot-pounds of torque at 4,000 rpm. *General Motors* torque at 4,000 rpm. While it doesn't possess the same low-level pulling power of the diesel, it has plenty of muscle to make freeway cruising a breeze.

"The H2 with the 6.0-liter Vortec has excellent on-pavement power, performance, and control for everyday driving and routine tasks like trailer towing," said GM Program Manager, Ken Lindensmith. "But its true character really shines in the off-road arena. It can easily soldier over rocks and through the harshest terrain."

Rather than being a compromise, the gas V-8 is well suited to the H2's on- and off-road mission and offers nearly the same versatility as the H1. The original, with

A Hummer H2 isn't afraid to get its feet wet: With as many as seven different ways to customize power delivery to wheels, it will get traction whether the river bottom is rocky or muddy. *Jim Fets/General Motors*

For tough work like rock climbing, the H2's drivetrain has such tricks as a drive-by-wire throttle that offers different response for different low-speed situations and the ability to lock the rear differential for maximum traction. *Jim Fets/General Motors*

its diesel engine and snorkel air intake, is legendary for its ability to ford streams 40 inches deep. The H2 is no slouch—with its conventional intake and spark ignition engine, it can attack a stream 20 inches deep at 5 miles per hour and 6 inches of water at 40 miles per hour and be none the worse for wear.

The 385 foot-pounds of torque is also more than a match for the H2's base curb weight of 6,400 pounds and has plenty of reserves to

enable the vehicle to climb 16-inch steps and rocks without getting hung up, and run over loose sand with remarkable ease.

The Vortec 6000 V-8 beneath the hood of the H2 is a descendent of GM's legendary small-block. It has a sturdy and durable, cast-iron block fitted with aluminum heads and sequential fuel injection. The overhead-valve configuration uses two valves per cylinder.

The cylinders have 4-inch bores, while the pistons have a stroke of 3.62 inches for an overall displacement of 364 cubic inches or 6.0 liters. The engine has a compression ratio of 9.4:1, which allows it to produce maximum power on regular 87 octane fuel.

Not only does the Vortec 6000 trace its roots to the small-block, it shares many design elements and construction techniques developed for the 2001 LS6 Corvette V-8 used in the high-performance Z06 model. These engines share the same deep-skirt iron block castings and utilize more efficient aluminum cylinder heads, which allow for better air flow. The re-engineered heads are 56 pounds lighter and have improved valve-seat durability over the heads used on the stock Corvette's LS1 engine. The Vortec 6000 heads also dissipate heat more quickly, which reduces overall cooling requirements and allows an increase in spark advance

The H2's four-wheel drivetrain's central transfer case routes power to the front and rear axles, where differentials split it between wheels. In high open mode, front/rear torque split is 40 percent/60 percent, while locked it is 50/50. *General Motors*

Typical Hummer terrain: up a steep incline in Moab, Utah, set in 4 LO with the differentials locked for the ultimate in both traction and torque delivery. *Jim Fets/ General Motors*

It's a bit hidden in there and takes a bit of reaching to get to, but this is the H2's 6.0-liter V-8, which shares roots, design features, and construction techniques with the Corvette Z06's high-performance engine. *John Lamm*

without pre-ignition, further enabling the engine to get the most out of low octane fuel.

The intake and exhaust ports are also identical to those in the LS6 head, for an increase in volumetric efficiency. The Vortec 6000 heads have a larger combustion chamber than the 5.7-liter LS6, which results in the larger 6.0-liter displacement. New, more durable, multi-layer steel (MLS) head gaskets maintain proper heat conductivity with the engine's cast-iron engine block.

A new steel camshaft, unique to the Vortec 6000, is the single biggest contributor to the increase in horsepower. The cam increases valve lift and duration slightly to take full advantage of the increase in volumetric efficiency allowed by the new cylinder head design. Performance improvements are also garnered with the addition of a lower-restriction exhaust system. A coil-near-plug ignition system delivers increased ignition energy, which in turn helps to reduce emissions and improve idle quality.

To get to the H2's engine, release the interior release handle, remove two exterior clips, then at the front of the hood, pull up and forward on hood-mounted handles, taking the hood to a vertical position. *Jim Fets/ General Motors*

The block has six-bolt main bearing caps, which adds to the overall rigidity. A stiff block is key to reducing the noise, vibration and harshness (NVH) levels of the powertrain. A new firing order also reduces stress by 7 percent on the internally balanced and counterweighted cast nodular iron crankshaft.

An advanced coolant loss protection system protects the engine in the event of coolant drainage, either partial or total. If a loss is detected, the computer limits engine power and allows the engine to run as an air-cooled system, giving the driver a limited ability to find a repair facility or suitable pull-off area. This so-called "limp-home" capability is a tremendous advantage in an off-road environment.

Components such as the alternator, power steering pump and air conditioning compressor are driven by a single serpentine belt.

The Vortec V-8 is equipped with a new Hitachi throttle-body injection system and is completely drive-by-wire;

there is no mechanical linkage between the accelerator pedal and the engine's induction system. This electronic drive-by-wire setup is actually a microprocessor that also monitors such items as transmission shift schedules or whether the transfer case is in high or low range and

Driver control for the H2's four-wheel drive system is via this dash-mounted panel, which allows the locking of the center and rear differentials for added traction.
John Lamm

decides what is the optimum throttle progression for these different operating modes.

The throttle progression has a setting that allows the driver to precisely control engine speed during very rough terrain driving. This revised throttle strategy is automatically engaged when the vehicle is in low. It allows the driver to step on the accelerator without opening up the throttle plate quickly or fully, reducing the chance for sudden or jerky power delivery when rock crawling. Even when pushed to the floorboard, the throttle will only deliver up to 75 percent of its normal capability. And getting to that limit takes longer, allowing the power to be delivered in more measured quantities.

When the vehicle is shifted into the high range on the transfer case, the engine delivers power in a normal fashion. A third configuration is "tow/haul," which alters the transmission shift points to provide smooth gear changes while the vehicle is under load.

The engine is mated to a heavy-duty 4L65E four-speed automatic transmission. The robust torque is quickly delivered to the wheels via a tall 3.06 first gear ratio, which allows the H2 to step out smartly. The remaining ratios are evenly spaced with a direct 1.00 ratio in third and a 0.69 overdrive for fourth.

The transmission drives all four wheels through a Borg-Warner two-speed electrically controlled transfer case. This system features a low range with a 2.64:1 ratio, which helps the vehicle in rock climbing. In high open mode, the transfer case delivers 40 percent of the torque to the front wheels and 60 percent to the rear. The differentials can be locked for an even 50/50 torque split.

The all-wheel-drive system has four operating positions plus neutral to provide a wide range of options for the driver. The high-range open or 4 Hi Open is used for normal driving on dry surfaces at any speed. There is a locked high range or 4 Hi Locked for semi-slippery surfaces, like rain, snow, or light sand. This locks the front and rear output shafts so they turn at the same speed, delivering equal amounts of torque fore and aft.

GM's design team shaped the H2's shift handle to look like an aircraft throttle control lever. Behind that lever is a heavy-duty 4L65E four-speed automatic transmission.
Jim Fets/General Motors

When the going gets slipperier or when the road ends, 4 Lo Locked is available. It not only locks the two prop shafts together, it engages the low 2.64:1 ratio in the planetary gear set, giving the equivalent of an extremely deep-ratio first gear and delivers maximum torque for slow-speed climbing. In addition to providing the different strategy for the drive-by-wire throttle response, this setting also allows the driver to select different mapping for the traction control system to better match the conditions encountered. The driver can switch the traction control over to TC2, which allows for a bit more wheel slip, which can help move the vehicle across snow or loose sand. While the normal traction control mode is tuned specifically for low grip on hard surfaces, TC2 is set up to provide maximum traction across unstable surfaces like sand, gravel, and deep mud. Engineers say this mode gives the H2 the ability to slip the wheels and "paddle" its way out of the loose material.

The fourth driving mode allows the driver to electrically lock the rear differential in 4 Lo, again providing the ultimate in torque delivery in low-speed operation across rocks or up severe inclines.

The three transfer-case options, two rear axle differential modes, and two Traction Control settings give the driver a total of seven different ways to customize power delivered to the wheels.

Like the diesel-driven H1, the H2, with its pushrod V-8, could be considered a throwback. But the advances in engine electronics, especially the use of drive-by-wire and coil-near-plug ignition as well as the advanced design of the cylinder heads, proves that the H2 is hardly antiquated. In fact, the OHV technology enables the H2 to produce most of its usable torque at low engine rpm, providing instantaneous response to throttle inputs. When coupled with the advanced two-mode traction control and an advanced transfer case with electrically locked rear differential, the Hummer H2 is proof positive that old and new technology can be combined in innovative ways to provide class-leading performance.

It's the H2's height that gives off its aggressive in-your-face attitude and tends to emphasize the Hummer's familiar boxy styling. The vehicle's size and weight make rooftop running lights a legal must. *John Lamm*

HANDS ON
THE H2

WALKING UP TO THE HUMMER H2 IMMEDIATELY DISPELS ANY NOTION THAT THIS IS A BABY HUMMER, ESPECIALLY WHEN AN H1 IS PARKED NEARBY.

The H1 has a low, mean, ground-hugging look; the H2 gets its aggressive in-your-face attitude from its height, which tends to accentuate Hummer's trademark boxy styling. If you're of average height and stand next to the front fender, the wheel opening will be at your armpit and the top of the hood at your shoulders. Looking up at the orange running lights at the top of the straight up-and-down windshield it seems as though they're perched on top of a mountain.

This height is overwhelming—the coil spring-equipped H2 stands at 79.2 inches compared to the relatively low-slung 75-inch-tall H1. It's not as wide at 81.2 inches compared to the original's width of 86.5 inches The H2 has a 122.8-inch wheelbase and is 189.8 inches long, or 5.3 inches longer than the H1.

A walk around the vehicle reveals many interesting details, some inspired by the original H1, others uniquely H2.

The face of the vehicle is pure Hummer, with inboard-mounted headlamps, outboard turn signals, and the traditional seven-slot grille, with the individual letters of HUMMER etched between each slot. The bright chrome finish, however, gives the H2 a flashy smile that can be muted by a choice of two different brush guards—one fits straight across, while the other, which is meant for extreme off-road use, wraps around the corners. Beneath the grille is a flush black bumper fitted with two huge auxiliary lights and a secondary air inlet. The lower half of this piece, which houses the front hitch receiver, extends under the vehicle and leads to a light gray metal skid plate embossed with the H2 logo.

Front and rear overhangs are relatively short, at 32.6 inches front and 34.6 inches at rear. Track is a wide 69.4 inches, front and rear.

The one-piece composite hood has additional grille-work on the top and has two pull handles inset on either side, a visual cue similar to H1's hood hooks.

The hood actually forms the front fenders that sport small blacked-out flares for the wheel arches. Two external latches also secure the hood, which has an internal release. Air boxes, one on each corner of the hood at the base of the windshield, add to the military-inspired styling.

Once the external latches are undone and the internal release pulled, the hood pops up slightly and can be

At the back, the H2 has a one-piece liftgate that is easy to operate and, when opened, provides a load area that is flush with the top of the bumper.
John Lamm

While the H2 is often known as the "Little Hummer," it is, in fact, taller than the H1 by 4.2 inches, and at 189.8 inches long is 5.3 inches longer than the original Hummer. *John Lamm*

The H2 grille with its seven openings is a tradition carried on from the original Willys Jeep. DaimlerChrysler tried to block its use by GM in the courts, claiming prior use on its Jeeps, but lost the case. *John Lamm*

tipped forward using the grab handles. It's a hefty piece requiring a bit of effort. The 6.0-liter V-8 engine is nestled into the cavernous engine bay and, despite the long reach from the sides, items such as the oil dipstick and fillers for engine oil, coolant, and windshield wiper fluid are well-marked and easily accessed.

From a distance, the front windshield looks flat, but when standing next to the H2 you notice that there is a gentle wraparound curve to the surface. Around to the side, the H2 sports popped-out door surfaces to mimic the H1, yet the detailing—like the optional chrome on the mirrors and door handles and the flush mounting of the glass—give the vehicle a more contemporary feel. H2 badging is fixed to the front doors, and the wheel-arch flares sweep down into the rocker area and back up over the rear wheel wells. Below the rocker panel, thick tubular steel bars that have been engineered to support the entire weight of the vehicle provide additional protection for the body. Two optional bolt-on step packages are available: one has individual steps for the front and rear doors, the second is a single running board providing front and rear access.

You can't help but notice the H2's huge wheels. The 17.0x8.5-inch alloy wheels have eight lug nuts fitted with LT315/70R17 Goodrich all-terrain tires. The wheel and tire combination stands nearly 3 feet tall.

In the right rear quarter panel, the H2 has an exposed gas cap, another styling cue from the H1. The roof is

Helpful in a vehicle as wide as the H2 are the remote-powered mirrors, which fold in electronically to make the Hummer a bit narrower for tight spaces whether in garages or on rock walls. *John Lamm*

equipped with rails that can be fitted with optional luggage rack crossbeams. The rear has a one-piece liftgate flanked by the taillamps and turn signals. Unlike the H2 concept that mounted the light clusters high on either side of the rear glass, these lights have been dropped down to flank the lower half of the rear hatch.

The liftgate is easy to operate and when opened, the rear load area is flush with the top of the rear bumper. Cargo floor height from the ground is 35.7 inches on coil spring models and 34.8 inches with air springs.

Embossed with the Hummer name, the rear bumper also features an integrated hitch receiver and is pre-wired for trailer lights. Two towing loops are standard. Again, the rear bumper extends beneath the bodywork to form a skid plate.

Inside the rear load area, a covered, full-size spare is vertically mounted on the left side of the bay, while an optional, third-row single-occupant seat can be folded down and flipped forward or removed entirely to provide additional load-carrying capacity. That third row offers 38.8 inches of headroom, 41.4 inches of shoulder room, 30.3 inches of hip room, and 27.3 inches of legroom.

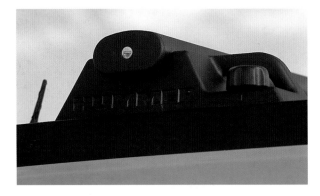

Rugged rooftop rails of the H2 are designed to take any number of optional luggage rack crossbeams and are lockable to discourage theft. *John Lamm*

Brush guards protect the H2's large rear taillights, while around the corner is another visual tie to the original Hummer H1, an exposed gas cap. *John Lamm*

Over-center clips firmly hold down the rear corners of the H2's large hood, while vents release hot air from the Hummer's engine compartment.
John Lamm

Design of the H2's interior retains some of the Hummer's military heritage, but softens and stylizes it for the consumer market, creating an efficient-yet-comfortable cockpit. *John Lamm*

The rear has 37.3 inches and 40 cubic feet of load space between the second row and the hatch and 71.7 inches when the rear seats are folded down.

The rear hatch area has a remote switch for the central locking system and when the vehicle is equipped with the optional air spring suspension, there is an outlet from the compressor that allows you to inflate anything from tires and balls to air mattresses.

The doors open with a handle pull and it's best to grab one of the six passenger compartment grab handles to pull yourself inside the cabin. The step-in height is a bit daunting, 24.9 inches front and 25.6 inches rear with the coil spring suspension, and 24.3 inches rear with the air suspension.

Sitting high above the ground at a thickly padded steering wheel, the view from the driver's seat is commanding.

The white-faced instruments are easy to see and nicely arranged with a large speedometer dominating the panel. A slightly smaller tachometer is placed to the left and there are five auxiliary gauges: water temperature, oil pressure, amps, fuel, and transmission oil temperature.

The power window switches are mounted in the door armrest and the outside rear-view mirrors have a power-folding feature that is activated by moving the mirror button to the neutral position. Holding the mirror button down to the right folds the mirrors in, pushing left moves them out.

A large center stack dominates the middle of the dashboard topped by two huge round air vents. The radio is positioned immediately below the vents with the climate controls and On Star buttons located at the bottom.

Along the left side of the center stack are the switches for the transfer case including 4 Hi and 4 Lo, the lock for the rear differential, a switch to engage the transmission's tow/haul mode and a button to engage the secondary traction control mode. On models equipped with the air suspension, there's also a switch for the extended rear ride height. The switches are well-marked and intuitive in operation. The windshield wipers are mounted on a steering column stalk, while a dash-mounted rotary switch controls the lights.

A large, chromed shift lever dominates the center console and looks like the throttle of a jet aircraft. There are large cup holders and a deep storage bin aft of the shifter; the bin has built-in racks for CD cases. The standard sound system features a single-play CD; an optional unit

Fitting for a heavy-duty vehicle, the H2's instrument panel is quite complete with not just speedometer and tachometer, but also fuel level, coolant temperature, oil pressure, transmission oil temp, and amp gauges. *John Lamm*

has a built-in six-disc changer. Built into the center console are three 12-volt power points for accessories.

The steering wheel has hands-on controls for the radio and heating/air conditioning system as well as switches for the cruise control and the information center located beneath the speedometer. The driver information center provides a way of customizing settings for two drivers, such as automatic door locking and lighting as well as providing warnings for up to 28 specific vehicle functions. The information center also acts as a trip computer, providing fuel economy and range, instantaneous fuel economy, two trip odometers and a function that keeps elapsed time and vehicle running hours.

There's also a roof-mounted console that houses the Home-link buttons for garage doors and home security lighting. H2s equipped with a large sunroof have a short console; vehicles without a sunroof have a longer unit that houses several flip-down storage bins for sunglasses and other small items.

The overall look is contemporary with just enough brightwork to give the cabin an upscale feel. The trim is a satin finish silver with gray tones, there's not a scrap of wood—real or fake—to detract from the business-like appearance. The only nit to pick is the use of exposed, bright hexi-head fasteners used for the trim panels. Not only does the bright color draw attention to them, you can see where the power driver marred the hex head. A change to a darker matte finish would help.

The power front buckets are comfortable and supportive and feature a multitude of power adjustments. The seats are equipped with center fold-down armrests, which are the same height as the ones on the door; when leather is specified, the package includes front and rear seat heaters.

The upright windshield is positioned far forward, adding to the spacious feel of the cockpit. The front row dimensions are generous: headroom is 40 1/2 inches, shoulder room is 66.4 inches, hip room is 62.9 inches, and legroom is 41.3 inches. The high seating position offers a commanding view of the road, and the relatively short greenhouse also imparts a secure feeling of being in a protected bunker.

The rear seat features a three-across bench, a huge departure from the H1's four-passengers-each-in-their-own-corner setup. At the rear of the console, there are two additional vents, a secondary control panel for the sound system, rear headphone jacks, and two more power points. The rear bench is comfortable, and features a center seating position, which also has a fold-down armrest with integrated cup holders and covered storage bin. All three rear seating positions are equipped with lap belts and shoulder harnesses.

Rear seat headroom is 39.7 inches, shoulder room is 66.3 inches, hip room is 62 inches, and legroom is 38.6 inches With the third-row single occupant seat, the H2 can comfortably carry six.

The rear seats are easily folded down, the seat bottoms flip up to allow the seatbacks to fold forward flat. Another nice touch are the headrests, which automatically fold rearward; there's no need to pull them out of the seatback and look for a place to store them. With the second row

Control center for the H2 driver is the steering wheel, which has a hefty grip, an airbag and six hands-on controls for such functions as radio station seek and volume.
John Lamm

The H2's center stack of controls shows the machine's General Motors heritage in the ergonomically efficient design and placement of its audio, climate, and drivetrain controls. The generous air vents are welcomed in hot weather. *John Lamm*

stowed and the optional third seat removed, the H2 has a cargo volume of 86.6 cubic feet.

On the safety front, the H2's first line of defense is its size and heft. Base curb weight is 6,400 pounds and the vehicle has an overall GVWR of 8,600 pounds. The stiff body structure and hydro-formed frame rails have been computer-designed to incorporate generous crumple zones to absorb impacts.

The H2 is also equipped with front airbags, along with a front passenger switch that allows the bag to be turned off when using a rear-facing child safety seat. The vehicle is also equipped with child safety-seat tether anchors in the rear.

In addition to the airbags and three-point belts in all seating positions, the Hummer H2 has been outfitted with soft trim panels, moldings, headliner, and other areas to protect from potential head injuries in collisions.

Security measures include the PASSLock anti-theft security system that uses rolling codes to ensure that the vehicle can be started with the proper key only. A standard anti-theft system also sounds the horn and flashes the lights if the vehicle is tampered with. Theftlock is also programmed into the radio, which remembers a portion of the vehicle's identification number. If stolen or removed from the vehicle, the radio won't operate and "locked" will show in the display. Also, the keyless remote fob has a panic button to sound the horn and flash the lights.

All H2s are equipped with retained accessory power, which can be programmed to allow the windows, radio, and sunroof to be operated up to 20 minutes after the vehicle has been turned off. The battery also features rundown protection, which automatically shuts the lights off if they've been left on for an extended time.

Despite its imposing stature, the H2 is not overly dramatic everyday operation. Unlike the H1, where you have to wait for the glow plug light to go out before firing up the diesel engine, the H2 starts the instant you twist the key. The 6.0-liter Vortec V-8 idles quietly and its smoothness is an indication of its seemingly effortless ability to produce 316 brake horsepower and 360 foot-pounds of torque.

The pedals are mounted directly in front of the driver, there's no-offset or wheel arch intrusion into the foot well, which has plenty of room for a dead pedal. The brake pedal is mounted slightly higher than the accelerator, you have to lift your foot off the throttle rather than slide it over to engage the brake.

There's a console-mounted hand brake that's easy to use, and the shifter has a beefy feel to it with well-defined gear detents. Pull the throttle-like shifter back into drive and you're off.

The H2's high seating position offers excellent visibility and the boxy shape lets you know exactly where the corners and the sides of the vehicle are at any time. This commanding outward view combined with the solid feel of the variable power-assisted recirculating ball steering contributes to the H2's ease of operation.

The ratio on the steering varies from 13:1 to 15:1, depending on vehicle speed, and it takes three full turns to move the steering wheel from lock to lock. The H2 has a turning radius of 43 1/2 feet.

A feature that would benefit a vehicle this size in an urban environment would be a rear proximity warning device to aid in parking maneuvers. The height of the vehicle, the dark tinting of the glass, and the vertical mounting of the spare tire make it somewhat difficult to see directly out the rear hatch, although the generous size

The H2's sturdy seats not only look the part, but also offer the type of support needed for off-roading and for short- or long-haul driving. *John Lamm*

There is plenty of rear seat room for three passengers, even hefty adults, while the seatbacks have a 60/40 split and can be folded to further increase cargo capacity. *John Lamm*

of the outside rear view mirrors somewhat compensates for this lack of direct rear ward visibility.

In the past, there have been irreconcilable differences with off-road prowess and good on-road manners. A soft, compliant suspension with a lot of wheel travel and a bit of steering wheel play is perfect for off-road rock climbing (the steering play is essential to prevent broken thumbs from wheel kickback). But this setup translates into vague, wallowing body motions on the highway. In addition, you find your head being tossed around from brake dive and excess body roll in corners, while all the time you're trying to figure out how to keep the vehicle centered in its lane. Conversely, a stiff suspension with crisp steering can deliver painful body blows to vehicle occupants when crashing over rocks and tree stumps in the back woods.

The Hummer H2 is proof that there needs to be no trade-off in ability versus comfort and control. The biggest surprise is the vehicle's on-road manners, which are most civilized. You'd expect that a vehicle that will go almost anywhere the H1 can go would be a bit soft, especially when you consider that the front shock absorbers have a travel of 10 inches.

With 46 mm monotube gas shocks front and rear, a front stabilizer bar of 36 mm and a rear 30 mm bar on the five-link rear suspension (air suspension models have an even stiffer 32 mm bar), the H2 has a taut, athletic feel on the tarmac. All the while, there's little sacrifice to ride comfort; the H2 is able to soak up road irregularities with aplomb.

The body-on-ladder frame construction of the H2 is the secret behind this ability. With a stiff structure that transmits little in the way of road noise, vibration and harshness, the vehicle can be tuned to provide a precise balance between good handling and extreme off-road capability.

For a vehicle as tall as the H2, it is remarkably stable in turns. Body roll is minimal and the steering turn-in is crisp and accurate. In turns, the H2 is neutral to slight understeer, which makes the vehicle predictable and forgiving when pushed hard. With the all-wheel-drive system delivering 40 percent of the torque to the front wheels under normal conditions and backed by traction control that's seamless in operation, the H2 delivers grip levels usually associated with cars.

In normal highway operation, the only vagaries to which the H2 is susceptible are crosswinds or turbulence from larger trucks. This is due primarily to the slab-sided nature of the Hummer design. Still, the H2 remains unflappable when dealing with such sudden gusts.

In the back seat, the center section between the outside seating positions can be lowered as a broad center console, providing a pair of generous cup holders.
John Lamm

While the suspension and steering do yeoman's work in making the H2 a daily driver, the heart of the Hummer—its V-8 power—cinches the deal. The factory estimates a 0 to 60 acceleration time of 9.9-seconds, which is a tremendous feat when you consider that H2 weighs twice as much as the average sedan. Promising fuel economy in the low teens, the H2 is equipped with a 32-gallon tank, good for more than 300 miles between refills.

That power is delivered transparently through the slick shifting four-speed automatic. At highway speeds, the transmission quickly kicks down into a lower gear when the accelerator is mashed to the floor. In addition to the positive gear changing, the transmission seems to know precisely which gear to be in with minimal hunting in or out of overdrive.

Just as the Hummer is relatively quick on its feet, it also possesses tremendous stopping power. The four-wheel disc brake system has 12.8-inch-diameter front and 13-inch-diameter rear rotors. The system also boasts four-channel ABS, dual-piston calipers, and dynamic brake proportioning. Stops are sure and well modulated thanks to good pedal feel and low effort.

Put it all together and the H2 fairly scoots down the road and feels much more nimble than its size would indicate. As easy as the H2 is to operate in the real world, the vehicle is simply amazing where the road stops.

On the south side of South Bend, Indiana, AM General owns 300 acres it has turned into a grueling off-road proving ground. It encompasses a paved track, dense, hilly woods, some wetlands, streams, and a small lake. In addition to testing the capabilities of the H1 and

Adding to the rugged mechanical/technical nature of the H2, designers shaped the transmission shift lever to look like the throttle levers of an airplane; the heft is a real advantage in off-road driving. *John Lamm*

H2, the proving grounds are also used to train military personnel in the fine art of off-roading.

There's a large field near the front of the property that resembles a parade lawn, until you take a closer look. Embedded in the lawn are several rock crevices patterned after certain sections of the Sierra Nevada's famed Rubicon Trail. Huge logs are strewn about, there's a sand pit, a cement hill peppered with craggy rocks and a long, 30-inch-deep water tank. And this is just a warm up for what lies beyond the tree line.

With GM's H2 Program Manager Kenneth Lindensmith seated beside me, I'm ready to see what this machine can do. Lindensmith advises me to shift the transfer case into the low range by putting the transmission in neutral first and then punching the dash button. A loud thunk emanates from beneath the H2, signifying that the lower gear range is engaged. For good measure, I hit the button that electrically locks the rear differential.

Sliding the gear lever into first, I ease onto the throttle and head for the cement hill. "It's best to approach these obstacles at an angle," Lindensmith instructs, "that way, the first part of the vehicle that makes contact is the tire." The hill is specifically designed to demonstrate the ability of the H2 to climb a 60-percent grade and traverse a 40-percent side slope.

The tire makes contact with the hill and I push harder on the accelerator. As the H2 begins to climb, the front windshield goes from being filled with a rock wall to clear blue sky as the nose points upward. I can feel the tremendous pull of the engine and the wheels begin to slowly walk from crag to crag without losing their grip. We reach the top of the peak and bottom out the vehicle, testing the 25.6-degree ramp break-over angle of the air spring H2 we're riding in. The vehicle briefly rests, then slides on the rocker protection, proving the point that the tube steel is strong enough to support the weight of the whole vehicle.

Lindensmith advises me to tap the brakes to settle the vehicle and then let go of the pedal, allowing the vehicle to walk itself down the other side. The engine braking of the V-8 does its job as we descend gently and with an approach angle of more than 40 degrees, the H2 is able to drive back out onto level ground without stubbing its nose.

Next we drive into the sand pit and engage the TC2 (traction control) mode. This allows some wheel spin without reducing engine torque. The H2 paddles along through the sand, retaining enough forward momentum to reach firmer ground.

Wheeling around sharply, I attack the logs, which are anywhere from 12 to 16 inches in diameter. Lindensmith explains that it's not speed, but rather precise wheel placement and well-modulated throttle control that wins the day off-road. Again, he advises an angled approach to the logs, allowing the vehicle to step over the obstacles wheel-by-wheel. On the larger logs, I feel contact between the floorpan and the wood. Lindensmith brushes it off saying the under-chassis protection is doing what it's designed to do.

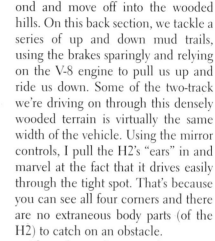

We finally reach the trailhead of the Rubicon. "This one requires a spotter," Lindensmith says, directing my attention to Doug, who's outside and properly attired for the role with a cowboy hat. Doug points out whether the steering wheel should be right or left, directing the wheels to be placed directly on top of the larger boulders and avoiding the crevices that could partially swallow the H2. This bit of rugged terrain demonstrates the value of the revised throttle control when the vehicle is in 4 Lo Locked. Only 75 percent of normal maximum throttle is delivered in this mode, and at a slower rate. This reduction in responsiveness actually increases the precision with which you can control the vehicle. As the H2 moves from rock to rock, I find that I'm able to deliver just enough power to climb up on top and then stop without having to use the brake. Taking my cue for the next move from the spotter, I can turn the wheel and feed in just enough throttle to gently ease the vehicle down then up the next boulder. It's an impressive display on how drive-by-wire electronics can improve the drivability of a vehicle in an extreme environment.

After we climb out of the Rubicon, Lindensmith suggests that I unlock the rear differential, upshift into second and move off into the wooded hills. On this back section, we tackle a series of up and down mud trails, using the brakes sparingly and relying on the V-8 engine to pull us up and ride us down. Some of the two-track we're driving on through this densely wooded terrain is virtually the same width of the vehicle. Using the mirror controls, I pull the H2's "ears" in and marvel at the fact that it drives easily through the tight spot. That's because you can see all four corners and there are no extraneous body parts (of the H2) to catch on an obstacle.

After descending another steep grade we run alongside a small lake until the trail stops at the shore. Lindensmith points to some poles sticking out of the water and says "that's our trail." I tentatively edge forward and we drive down into the water. We ford through nearly 2 feet of water, the closest I've ever been in my life to being in an amphibious vehicle. The H2 pushes the H2O aside and motors up the far bank. We've driven about an eighth of a mile through a lake. Once back at the infield, I note that the water was above the bottom shut-line for the doors yet we were bone dry. That little demonstration alone is proof that the H2, with its civil road manners and off-road athleticism, is clearly in a class of its own.

H2s with air suspension have an air inflator in the cargo area that allows tire pressures to be altered in the field. For example, after dropping pressure for running in sand, the driver can boost it for hard surfaces. *John Lamm*

An important feature of the H2 factory is an off-road course for testing the Hummers that includes a water crossing for checking the vehicle's 20-inch fording depth. *Jim Fets/General Motors*

CHAPTER 7

FAST-TRACK FACTORY

IT'S NOT SURPRISING THAT THE HUMMER H2 HAS AMAZING ABILITIES ON- AND OFF-ROAD—GIVEN THE VEHICLE'S LINEAGE. IT NEATLY COMBINES GM'S EXPERTISE IN BUILDING FULL-SIZE LUXURY TRUCKS AND AM GENERAL'S VAST EXPERIENCE IN MAKING VEHICLES THAT CAN CONQUER EXTREME TERRAIN.

What isn't apparent is the speed with which the H2 came to market, not just from a design and development standpoint, but also from a manufacturing perspective. It is simply amazing that in early 2002 H2s began rolling off the line at AM General's headquarters in Mishawaka, Indiana, from a factory that didn't exist barely a year earlier. Besides setting records for speed, the Hummer H2 plant is special because it represents the latest in lean manufacturing and is a test bed for techniques that will likely become the industry standard.

This new state-of-the-art plant almost didn't happen on time because of "Area 51." Far from the secret military installation in Nevada, the Area 51 that concerned AM General in the early months of 2000 was a neighborhood of 51 homes on a tract of land located immediately to the east of the H2 plant site. Although the plant itself wouldn't infringe on the neighborhood, AM General needed the additional buffer zone acreage for parking and vehicle shipping. And besides, who would want to live next to an 80-foot-tall structure that would block the sun half the day?

But because of the secret negotiations between AM General and GM, there was no way the Hummer people could approach these homeowners to lay the necessary groundwork to acquire the property.

Once the deal became public, and a timetable for the new plant announced, AM General President Jim Armour had a crisis brewing in Area 51. The homeowners thought the new plant would be owned and operated by General Motors and it was their understanding when the January announcement was made that they needed to be out of their homes by May.

"It was a real mess," Armour recalled. "We had all sorts of activists, media, and lawyers involved." It looked as if the H2 plant was about to become bogged down in a legal quagmire.

Knowing no other way to address the issue than take a direct approach, Armour invited all the homeowners to a meeting at AM General headquarters, located in the H1 plant adjacent to the new factory site.

Armour spoke directly and candidly to the homeowners. "I told them first off that no one had to be out by May, because that was the timetable when we were beginning construction of the new plant on our property." He also explained to them the nature of AM General's agreement with GM and that it wasn't the auto giant that was building the plant or looking to force them out of their homes. Armour also stressed the fact that the new plant would create jobs that were sorely needed in the area. Finally, he opened the books to them. "I wanted to show them that there's no way they're going to be paid way more than fair market value for their properties, we simply didn't have the cash," Armour said.

His straight talk paid off. Over the course of the next eight months, deals were struck with all the homeowners, the houses were leveled and the plant and its grounds completed on time and on budget. During the plant dedication, a special time was set aside for the homeowners to visit the plant and see for themselves what they had helped to make a reality. Armour said that 47 of the 51 homeowners came. In the plant's administration building,

Home of the Hummer is this sprawling facility in Mishawaka, Indiana. As part of its agreement with AM General, GM built a new specifically for H2 assembly. *AM General*

Hummer headquarters in Mishawaka, Indiana, home to the H1 and site of negotiations between AM General and GM that led to the creation of the H2. *AM General*

H2 doors and hoods are completed on a parallel line to the body, then attached later in the assembly process, facilitating the assembly of all pieces. *AM General*

H2s go through a "ro-dip" electrolysis tank to apply undercoating. This unique system turns the vehicle while it's being coated eliminating air trapped beneath horizontal body panels, giving them a uniform layer of undercoating.
AM General

there's a leaded glass door from one of the homes to serve as a reminder of the neighborhood that once stood on the plant property.

What the homeowners saw on their tour was a sparkling 630,000-square-foot plant adjoining the 570,000-square foot H1 plant. The entire AM General operation covers 131 acres, including the 35 acres from Area 51. The building was built in about 14 months with a safety record far better than industry averages, Armour pointed out

proudly. On the job site, there were only 2.3 lost-work-day cases per hundred workers recorded by the Occupational Safety and Health Administration (OSHA) compared to the prevailing 8.3-day average for Indiana.

The plant began operation with 660 workers on one shift. By the end of 2002, the second shift was expected to be in full swing, bringing total employment to just over 1,200 workers, producing between 40,000 and 46,000 H2s annually.

There are three zones to the plant. At one end is the body shop anchored by 46 dock doors that receive 103 tractor trailer loads per day with components from 281 suppliers. The middle and tallest section of the facility is the paint shop, while the third area houses final assembly. Although the plant is organized around lean manufacturing techniques, that doesn't mean the H2 plant favors robots over humans. "Most assembly plants have anywhere from 350 to 450 robots doing various jobs," Armour explained, adding "we have only 24 robots."

There are several reasons why; the first being volume. Even though 40,000 vehicles seems to be a huge number, most auto manufacturers that rely extensively on automation produce vehicle runs in the hundreds of thousands per year. The high cost of acquiring and maintaining robots for such a limited run of vehicles as the H2 didn't make economic sense. The automation that is used in the plant is reserved for jobs that are dangerous, dirty or time consuming.

The philosophy behind lean manufacturing calls for minimal inventory via just-in-time deliveries and workers organized into small teams. The underlying tenet is that problems are solved where they occur rather than being sent down the line for someone else to tackle. If a given task hasn't reached 70-percent completion by the time the conveyor has moved to a fixed point three-quarters

through the station, the worker pulls a yellow cord that sounds a chime specific to that location. The chime summons additional help to complete the task or address any problems that have cropped up in the process. If the vehicle reaches the end of the workstation and the problem hasn't been corrected, the red cord is pulled, stopping the line in that sector of the plant.

The tour of the H2 plant starts in the body shop where the metal panels are welded into bodies. Except for one

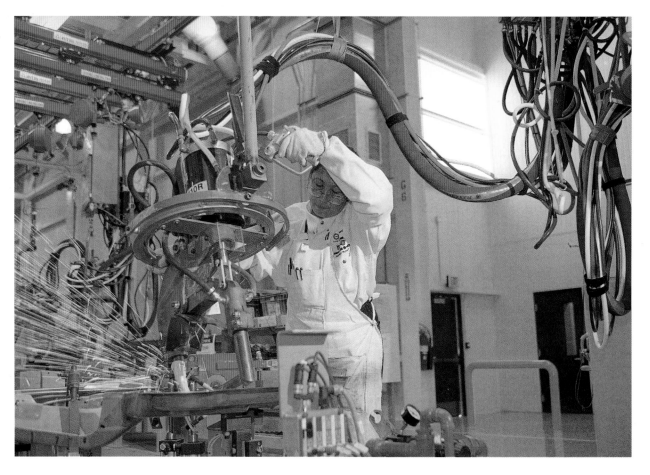

It is anticipated that after production ramp-up is completed, the new GM-built assembly line will employ just over 1,200 workers, producing 40,000 to 46,000 H2s each year. *AM General*

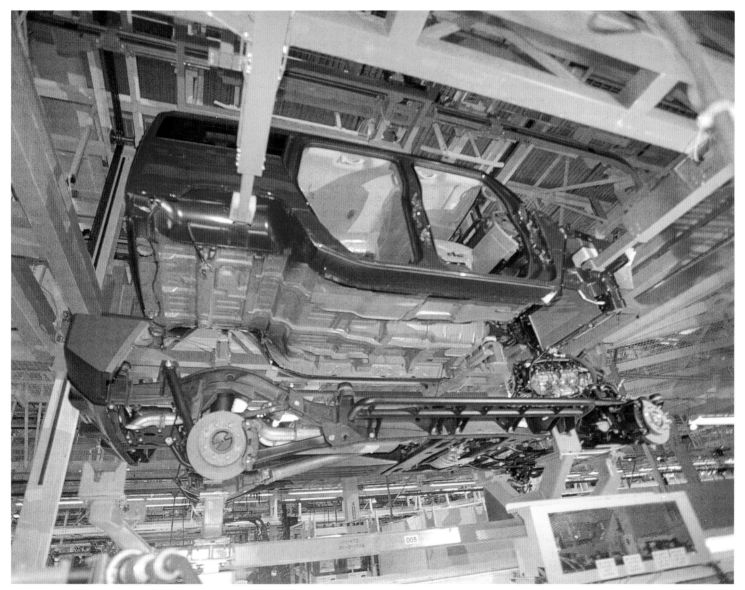

In the automated body drop, the finished body is positioned over the completed chassis, then they are "married" as the H2 approaches the end of the assembly line. *AM General*

large automated welding fixture, most of the work, which includes 3,600 spot welds on each body, is done manually, which gives the H2 a hand-crafted aura. Lasers inspect each body to ensure proper alignment of the panels and gaps before the shell is sent along.

Besides adhering to lean manufacturing tenets, there are other techniques and equipment employed that reflect the plant's relatively small footprint. Two examples are the use of elevators to move the bodies up and down through the paint shop and assembly line as well as the unique "ro-dip" tank for the undercoat—"ro" meaning rotary operation.

In a traditional e-dip operation, vehicles are pulled down through a long electrolysis tank for the undercoat. All Hummer H2s are dipped nose first and somersaulted

H2 chassis assembly takes place at waist level, making it easier for workers to attach components; the frame is flipped over so workers can easily add pieces to the chassis.
AM General

through a shorter but deeper tank. The vehicle is actually zapped by electrolysis when it's upside down.

Ro-dip has two benefits. The first is the compact space of the operation and the second, by turning the vehicle over, eliminates the chance of air being trapped beneath the horizontal body panels, which would result in a thinner application of undercoating.

After the vehicle re-emerges from the ro-dip tank it enters the four-story-tall paint shop. An elevator takes it to the second floor where the body is manually prepped and then painted by 17 robot arms, which apply 5 gallons of paint and clearcoat per vehicle. The freshly painted shell, with the composite hood and doors in place, is lifted to the third floor ovens where the finish is

Nearing the end of the assembly line, a Hummer H2 needs only to have its doors added and then go through a number of quality audits that ensure well-made H2s. *AM General*

After being run briefly on a chassis dynamometer and going through a high-pressure water bath as a check against leaks, a just-finished H2 is driven from the factory to a short track test.
AM General

cured. The fourth floor of the paint shop houses the air filtration and heating equipment for the ovens.

When the body leaves the paint shop, the doors and hood are removed to facilitate final assembly. They travel along with the body on a separate conveyor.

As the body enters the final assembly hall, work begins on the H2's chassis on a second parallel line. The frame enters the line upside down at waist level to make it easy for workers to affix components. The axles and skid plates are attached and then a special jig that fits into the front and rear hitch receivers automatically flips the frame over. Meanwhile, the drivetrain funnels over from a separate line where the engine is dressed and mated to the transmission and transfer attached. Swung over to the line on an overhead lift, the drivetrain is dropped onto the righted frame.

Across the alleyway, workers install the body hardware, seats and instrument panels, while the windshield is mounted in one of the few automated operations in final assembly.

Although major components like the body panels, engine block, and transmission come into the plant from outside suppliers, there is still a high concentration of assembly work actually done in the plant instead of relying on pre-assembled modules.

Part of that reason is the unique labor agreement reached between AM General and UAW Local 5. (The oldest existing UAW local in the country, it was originally formed to represent workers at South Bend-based Studebaker.) Armour negotiated a 10-year work agreement compared to the industry norm of three years. In addition, there are only five job classifications, and workers are allowed to move around from job to job. Although workers at the adjoining H1 plant were given the opportunity to move over to the new H2 plant, only 78 transferred. The balance of the workforce is new and has undergone 177,000 hours of training prior to the startup of full production.

Because this innovative agreement fixes labor costs for such a long period of time, AM General wants to do as much work as it can in-house. Items like the instrument panel, which usually arrive in one piece, are actually assembled on-site.

As the vehicle nears the end of the line, the finished body is again hoisted to the second level via elevator where it is positioned over the completed chassis for the automated body drop. Again, the drop occurs at waist level, which enables the workers to bolt the vehicle together without having to bend over or work in a pit.

The H2s are driven off the assembly line onto a dynamometer, where the vehicle is started and run briefly. Then it's moved over to a long, enclosed line that looks like a car wash, except that the water comes out at a much higher pressure to allow the workers to check for leaks in the seals.

Another area is used for quality audits where vehicles are pulled from the line at random for a complete inspection. Just outside the rear door of the factory is a small garage with a computer-controlled shake test. A vehicle can be placed with its tires on four large rams that allow the operator to bump and shake the vehicle, testing for loose body and trim panels as well as squeaks and rattles.

All Hummer H2s are given a final dynamic test with a quick run through a test track before being moved to the shipping lot.

Despite being built and put into operation in record time, the H2 plant has the look of a well-established, smooth running, state-of-the-art factory. As evidenced by the high build quality of the first units coming out of the plant, no corners were cut. And for those first H2 owners who anxiously awaited the delivery of the vehicles in late summer of 2002, they owe a little extra thanks to some people they'll never know: the homeowners who decided to move aside for progress.

Although designed to be very capable off-road, the Hummer H2 also is an excellent urban machine, where its image of power and strength make it popular, as do its road manners and comfort level. *Jim Fets/General Motors*

MAKING THE SALE

SELLING THE HUMMER H2 SHOULD BE A NO-BRAINER. IT HAS LOOK-AT-ME STYLING; GO-ANYWHERE, DO-ANYTHING CAPABILITIES; AND THE ENDORSEMENT OF A HUGE HOLLYWOOD STAR: ARNOLD SCHWARZENEGGER. BEST OF ALL, IT WAS LAUNCHED INTO A RED HOT LUXURY SUV MARKET WITH A LIST PRICE OF $48,800, MUCH LESS THAN THE RANGE ROVER OR LINCOLN NAVIGATOR AND ABOUT THE COST OF A LOADED SUBURBAN.

That $48,800 included an impressive array of standard equipment, including such functional bits as four-wheel drive, locking rear differential, four-wheel disc brakes, and traction control. H2s also carry an impressive array of creature comforts such as a standard nine-speaker Bose audio system with AM/FM stereo and single CD player, remote keyless entry, cruise control, power seats, dual zone climate control, and OnStar communications system. Only two option packages were offered. The Lux Series, priced at an additional $2,575, included an upgraded sound system with six CD in-dash changer,

The beefy front section of the Hummer's frame allowed GM's first standard winch receiver, which is designed to accommodate a 9,000-pound winch. The mount for the receiver is built into the frame's front cross member. *Jim Fets/ General Motors*

heated leather seats, chrome appearance package, tubular assist steps, and custom carpet mats. The Adventure Series, which cost $2,215, included the air spring rear suspension, brush guard, first aid kit, tool kit, portable lamp, six-disc in-dash CD changer, roof rack crossbars, and customer carpet floor mats.

One price, two optional packages. Michael C. DiGiovanni, general manager of Hummer, only wishes life were so simple. At the end of the day, for all the attention the H2 will draw, it still is a $50,000 vehicle.

And people spending that kind of money are special and expect to be treated that way.

Granted, one of the reasons why General Motors went to such great lengths to secure the Hummer nameplate is the vehicle's almost mythical allure to youngsters. The Hummer H1, and now the H2, is as recognized and as popular a pinup among adolescents as the Lamborghini Diablo. Of course, youngsters aren't likely to smash open their piggy banks, march down to the local Hummer dealer, and plunk down nearly $50,000 in change to buy

Always a popular accessory with the sport-utility crowd, polished wheels will be part of the package for many H2 owners. *Jim Fets/General Motors*

one. But it certainly doesn't hurt to have the GM name associated with a vehicle like the H2 for future reference when these kids eventually enter the new car market.

So if you're not selling Hummer to kids, who are your buyers and how do you sell it?

DiGiovanni broke the process down into three main tasks, the first of which was building the dealer network to make purchasing convenient for consumers. Next he set about positioning the Hummer brand in the market, which includes identifying potential customers. Finally, he needed to pull together the advertising campaign and roll out the product.

When the tie-up between GM and AM General was announced, there were several divisions and their dealers within the auto giant that wanted to link up with Hummer, like the tie-up in the past between Pontiac and GMC. DiGiovanni went against tradition and insisted that Hummer be a stand-alone operation and would select only the best GM dealers with the highest customer satisfaction ratings, good employee morale, and a track record of profitability in key locations.

Initially, dealers are required only to set aside a portion of their showrooms for H1 and H2, but a separate building will be required once the division adds an H3 in the lineup. There also needs to be a dedicated service write-up area, although the garage where the actual work is done can be shared with other makes.

Hummer has developed a template for a typical dealership, so that the look and feel of all retail points are consistent. The design incorporates a curved roof inspired by the Quonset hut to recall the vehicle's military heritage. The floor plan is open and inviting and there's extensive use of exposed beams, rods, and wires. This so-called tensile architecture, in which the actual building supports become part of the visual appeal, fits in with the high-tech nature of the vehicles.

In addition to the showroom floor, there is a dedicated service area and a boutique for dealer-installed accessories as well as clothing, watches, and gear associated with the Hummer lifestyle. Dealers are also given a wide range of add-on accessories for the H2, including wrap-around brush grille guards, off-road spotlights (both roof- and brush guard-mounted), tubular taillamp guards, a hard cargo carrier for the roof, assist steps, and various floor and cargo area mats.

Outside, the plan calls for an off-road course that will enable sales personnel to give demonstration rides and provide buyers with orientation on the off-road operation and capabilities of both the H1 and H2.

"A Hummer needs to be authentic," said DiGiovanni, explaining the use of the understated industrial look rather than building a typical luxury car showroom with plenty of marble. He also cited that the ability to have a bit of rugged, off-road terrain on which to exercise the vehicles adds to that authenticity.

As DiGiovanni was developing the dealer network with Sales Manager Steve Hill, he also began the process of identifying the Hummer customer base and developing a strategy to reach them.

Those H2 roof racks aren't just for looks; they can be put to practical use with such extras as carriers for mountain bikes and pods for carting along extra gear and equipment.
Jim Fets/ General Motors

The starting point was Hummer H1 owners. These buyers are highly affluent empty nesters who own an average of six-plus vehicles, ranging from classic cars to Rolls-Royces and even pickup trucks. "They typically bought H1 in lieu of another vehicle or an exotic vacation or a home addition," DiGiovanni explained. "We designed the H2 for a more mainstream group of buyers."

Working with Hummer Marketing Director Marc Hernandez, their research concluded that Hummer has two extreme characteristics—functionality and exclusivity—which appeal to two distinct groups. The two groups identified by Hernandez includes Rugged Individualists, who want the Hummer because of its off-road abilities, and Successful Achievers, who can afford a Hummer because it is the best vehicle of its type.

Exclusivity is merely icing on the cake for the first group, who tend to be small business owners and tradesmen who have done very well. The second group tend to be extremely affluent buyers who want to make a statement or drive an attention-getting vehicle. The underlying off-road functionality of the original Hummer adds to the aura of distinction.

"In practical terms, the Rugged Individualist will be more likely to take it off-road and exploit all capabilities," Hernandez noted. "Successful Achievers are more likely to drive it on-road as a symbol of their daring and success.

"Our challenge with the H2 is to appeal to both groups without alienating them," Hernandez explained. In fact, the two luxury option packages, Lux and Adventure, were tailored specifically with these two sets of buyers in mind. Most important of all, Hernandez stressed, the vehicle had to deliver on its promise of performance.

These two groups seemed to have little in common, then Hernandez discovered that there were several traits that overlapped. Both liked the bold, in-your-face styling of the Hummer; they tended to be irreverent and were, in their own ways, risk takers. The Rugged Individualists took risks in their leisure activities, like off-roading and other

Stepping up and into an H2 can be a reach for some drivers and passengers, who will appreciate the accessory steps that can be attached to the sill bars. *Jim Fets/General Motors*

outdoor sports; Successful Achievers were risk takers in their professional lives.

The word that both groups responded to was *daring*. DiGiovanni and Hernandez used this word to describe what they call the "House of Hummer."

Hernandez explained that several other key words and concepts were used to support this Daring theme and will reflect the way Hummer approaches business. They are:

Exclusive. The H2 can be built in volumes of 40,000 to 46,000 per year. But taken as a percentage of an SUV market that tops three million annually, Hummer owners aren't likely to become ubiquitous any time soon. Even

Off-roading can take the H2 through rugged territory, so brush guards that prevent damage to lights and other accessories are an important part of the machine.

Jim Fets/General Motors

The front and rear hitch receivers can be put to several good uses, such as a step-up to reach the top of the H2.

Jim Fets/General Motors

after variations of the H2 are added to the line, like the SUT and a third, smaller H3, DiGiovanni didn't see Hummer selling over 200,000 units in the foreseeable future, ensuring a measure of exclusivity will remain.

Extreme Design. The in-your-face, aggressive look of the Hummer with its flat windscreen, huge wheels, and sharply chiseled body is the essence of Hummer's popularity. While future designs may explore new areas for the marque, it will never be another "me-too" SUV, Hernandez promises.

Irreverent. DiGiovanni expected the advertising campaign and even events sponsored by Hummer to have a touch of irreverence. Hummer's advertising manager, Liz Vanzura—lured away from Volkswagen (VW)—retained an agency formed by executivess from the group responsible for VW's successful campaigns which helped lift the German automaker's U.S. sales and increase its popularity in the youth market.

Best in Class. The Hummer team fervently believed that the Hummer must always be able to do exactly what

Extra powerful lighting is another popular add-on for off-roaders, and the H2 option list includes both roof- and brush-guard-mounted lamps. *Jim Fets/ General Motors*

When it comes to sales, Michael C. DiGiovanni is the man in charge of building the new dealer network, positioning the H2 in the market, and launching this important new product. *General Motors*

General Motors will have 150 new Hummer dealerships for selling both the traditional H1 and the new H2. This prototype dealership will be on a five-acre plot of land called, "an adult amusement park."
General Motors

the looks promise. If it can't, the allure of owning the vehicle will vanish quickly. While the vehicles will always look extreme, the idea of Best in Class off-road ability will also drive the appearance of future models. They will continue to have short front and rear overhangs, excellent ground clearance and full-time four-wheel-drive.

The final pillar in the house of the Hummer is the idea that owning one is an experience. Going places and doing things, especially off-road, will always be a part of owning a Hummer. It starts with the off-road course at the dealership and may end up halfway around the world on special trips and off-road opportunities sponsored by Hummer or the Hummer Owner's Club.

And while some of the fun in Hummer ownership seems to be related to a certain amount of swagger, DiGiovanni also pointed out that many H1 owners donate the use of the vehicles and time to help out in rescue efforts,

flood and storm relief and other charity work. "I expect this kind of volunteerism will continue with the H2," DiGionvanni said. In addition, both the factory and the owner's club promote responsible off-roading through such programs as Tread Lightly.

Still, Hummer will always be about fun and passion. The off-road capability may provide the rationale for what is purely an emotional, gotta-have-it vehicle. Having both the H1 and H2 in the same showroom will give dealers a powerful one-two punch.

"The Hummer H1 will live on, its awesome reputation intact, and the H2 will expand the brand's offerings, bringing the Hummer mystique to a wider audience," DiGiovanni predicted. "While we'll eventually offer a full portfolio of products, at its core, Hummer is and will remain an extremely powerful brand that connects to consumers on a decidedly emotional level."

There's much more to the GM/AM General alliance than the Hummer H2 wagon. It is an unusual partnership, and you can expect it to yield unusual future products. *John Lamm*

THE NEXT BIG THING

ONE OF THE FAVORITE CATCH PHRASES OF AUTO EXECU-
TIVES THROUGHOUT THE WORLD IS "WE DON'T LIKE TO
DISCUSS FUTURE PRODUCT."

The future is usually a closely guarded secret, unless a manufacturer is in big trouble and figures the best way to get some positive ink is to let the world know about the exciting products it has in the pipeline.

On the other hand, the public—as soon as it's had its fill of a particular fad—seems to say, "What have you done for me lately?" There is an almost insatiable demand for "The Next Big Thing."

As illustrated by the story of the H2 and the unique partnership between General Motors and AM General, the Hummer isn't a typical automotive operation. So true to form, Hummer let the public in on its future by showing the next iteration of the H2 well over a year before the wagon went on sale.

The Hummer H2 SUT was the surprise hit of the 2001 New York Auto Show. None other than Arnold Schwarzenegger and New York Mayor Rudolph Giuliani introduced the truck out in the middle of Times Square. As part of the debut, Hummer ponied up $13 million as a sponsor of Schwarzenegger's Inner City Games, a charity that sponsors sports and academic programs and awards scholarships in urban schools.

The H2 SUT was a significant vehicle on two counts. It showed that like the H1, which is offered in four civilian body styles ranging from a two-seat soft-top pickup to a four-seat wagon, the H2 will be offered in a number of different models. Secondly, the SUT, unlike the original H2 concept, was based on the same modified GMT-800 platform components and sheet metal as the production model.

The SUT is an interesting study in the evolution of the H2 from concept to production vehicle. All the surfaces are the same as the new H2, but the body detailing, which eliminates the exposed hinges and other pieces of brightwork, still has some body jewelry not found in production. For instance, the hood latch has been changed from metal on the SUT to plastic. The production H2 has only chromed door pulls as part of the optional chrome package, the SUT has brushed aluminum handles and bezels. But the SUT is the same in the presentation of the

At the 2001 New York Auto Show, actor and Hummer fan Arnold Schwarzenegger and New York Mayor Rudolph Giuliani were on hand to unveil the next new Hummer, the H2 SUT or Sport-Utility Truck. *General Motors*

front bumper, the black plastic flare that runs from the wheel wells through the rocker panel, the tubular rocker protection, and the design of the wheels.

The SUT is expected to be launched as early as 2004 and will feature the concept's unique mid-gate arrangement that expands the utility of the vehicle's small cargo bed. The vehicle has a power rear window that can be lowered into the rear bulkhead. When the rear seat is flipped forward, that bulkhead can be dropped down to floor level, opening up the entire rear of the vehicle, giving it enough room to carry a 4x8-foot sheet of plywood.

The concept SUT was also shown with a bike rack, which will most likely be a dealer-installed option, and a bit of high tech gadgetry that probably won't see production, a 360-degree night vision system. Other bits that will see production are GPS navigation and 110 volt outlets in addition to the numerous 12-volt power points. The interior of the concept is also a fairly faithful representation of the current H2 interior. It's likely that there will be few changes inside the SUT when it bows.

Beyond the SUT, however, Hummer officials are coy. There has been some work done on a four-door pickup with a much longer standard bed than the SUT.

One particular military variant under discussion is the slant back of the H1, which works quite well with that vehicle's wide track and low stance. However, because of the taller and narrower proportions of the H2, there is some concern that a slant-back version of the newest Hummer, instead of resembling the H1 military model, might come off looking more like the Pontiac Aztek, which hardly can be called a sales success. It's a safe bet that there isn't a slant back on the drawing boards.

Besides new body styles, both the H1 and H2 lend themselves to customization. As early as June 2002, aftermarket tuners who participated in the Specialty Equipment Marketing Association (SEMA), which has an annual trade show in Las Vegas in November, were taking delivery of H2s with an eye to creating personalized

GM has shown how serious it is about expanding the H2 line by its early showing of the four-door pickup SUT, with the concept vehicle based on the same type of GMT-800 chassis as the production H2 wagon. *General Motors*

expressions of the ultimate SUV. Already in the works are two H2s that take the Hummer concept to opposite extremes. The first is a modified, super-tough H2 designed to conquer the Baja 1000. Being developed by famed desert racer Rod Hall, this H2 will sport a multiple shock set up, a raised body, and a stripped-down interior. You can be sure there will be brush guards and auxiliary lights galore and a patriotic red, white, and blue paint scheme.

The other model, by automotive designer Bruce Canepa, is an executive express. Think of it as part street rod/part SUV. Canepa says this special edition SUV, which will be offered through the dealers in limited numbers, boasts an inter-cooled supercharger that will boost the 6.0-liter Vortec's output to 500 hp. Special paint, blacked-out windows, and custom exterior body parts will complement the 20-inch wheels shod in special 36-inch-tall Michelin tires with 16-inch brake rotors. The interior will sport custom, five-bar diamond-plate-style leather and titanium accents. A custom sound system will be pre-wired for a host of plug-in accessories ranging from a DVD player to an electronic game console.

Beyond customization of the H1 and H2, as well as adding the SUT and other variants to the H2 model lineup, there is very real talk of an H3, which would be critical in allowing the distribution network, the dealerships, to stand alone as separate franchises.

The H3 will be built on a slightly smaller derivation of GM's mid-size Chevy Trailblazer/GMC Envoy SUV platform that will underpin Chevy's new Colorado pickup, which replaces the S-10. The Colorado architecture uses an in-line five-cylinder version of the 270-horsepower 4.2-liter in-line six found in the Trailblazer/Envoy.

The unique off-road ability of Hummer may be one of the reasons why the Colorado underpinnings are favored over Trailblazer for the H3. The shorter five-cylinder powerplant would reduce the front overhang,

Planned for the 2004 model year, the H2 SUT will be the perfect mate for the H2 wagon, offering go-anywhere capability with everyday civility. *General Motors*

allowing the H3 to have a high approach angle, critical in extreme conditions.

Look for the H3 styling to be a continuation of the H1/H2 theme—sharp-angled and boxy with a flat windscreen. Hummer insiders indicate that this new model, which would be a true "Baby Hummer," would be built at a GM plant, be priced at about $28,000-plus, and sell in volumes of just over 100,000. It should see production in 2005 or 2006.

Even further out is a possible H4. Word is that a concept for this vehicle is currently in the works at GM, but that the company pulled back from plans to show the vehicle in 2003 for fear it would undercut an announcement of H3 production, which is expected by the end of 2002. Early indications are that the vehicle will be an open-top entry-level vehicle priced below the H3.

One official hinted that a GMC show vehicle called the Terracross, which was unveiled at the North American International Auto Show in January 2001, is worth a closer look because it shows an approach that might be considered for the H4.

Although quite modern in its overall execution, the Terracross has the same kind of proportions that distinguish the Hummer H1. Instead of being tall, it's wide. It retains the same sort of short front and rear overhangs that promise high approach and departure angles. The squared-off wheel arches, low greenhouse, and aggressive face definitely have a Hummer-like feel.

Unlike the H1 and H2, which have body-on-frame construction, the Terracross is a unit-body based on GM's new mid-sized Epsilon platform. The Epsilon is primarily a front-drive chassis destined for service as the

The H2 SUT has the same "mid-gate" used in several GM pickups, allowing the rear window to drop and the rear bulkhead to be lowered to create a larger pickup bed. *General Motors*

The interior of the SUT concept is basically the same as the production H2, with added brightwork. One trick not likely to see production was a prototype 360-degree night vision system. *General Motors*

In addition to future models, expect the H2 wagon to go through continual development that will expand uses for the rugged Hummer.
John Lamm

next generation Opel Vectra, Saab 9-3, and Chevy Malibu. It is expected to spawn some all-wheel-drive variants, including several so-called "crossover" vehicles that combine SUV styling with passenger car build quality and refinement. The Terracross was designed with this crossover market in mind. One interesting design feature of the vehicle is its suicide door arrangement and lack of a B-pillar.

There's nothing remarkable about the Terracross' 112.9-inch wheelbase and 171.9-inch overall length. It gets its Hummer-like wide-shouldered stance from its height of just 63.7 inches and width of 75 inches. There's

nothing remarkable about its engine—it's powered by a 3.4-liter V-6 rated at just 185 brake horsepower and 205 foot-pounds of torque, the same engine that is found in the Pontiac Aztek and Buick Rendezvous.

Could a vehicle like the Terracross be a Hummer? As presented, no, because it lacks the extreme off-road capability required of the marque. That's not to say that a unit-body, all-wheel-drive vehicle with a six-cylinder engine someday can't be a Hummer.

The important thing to look at is the shape of the Terracross. The highly machined, sharp-edged styling is very clean and modern and yet the proportion is pure

GM debuted the Hummer H2 SUT at the 2001 New York Auto Show—setting its debut in Times Square—and creating the surprise hit of the show.
General Motors

At the 2001 Detroit Auto Show, GM showed another Hummer-like concept, the GMC Terracross, which could be a look at a future type of unit body Hummer variation. *General Motors*

Given the enthusi-asm for the Hummer H1 and H2, it's apparent that there is a golden future ahead for the products of the unusual corporate partnership between GM and AM General.
John Lamm

Hummer. While hard-core off-roaders insist on body-on-frame construction, that's not to say that a unit-body vehicle can't be built rugged enough to perform well in that environment. Just like the AM General people were shown that a five-link live axle can perform as well as an independent rear, perhaps a unit-body vehicle can set a new standard. Certainly the powertrain would have to be beefed up; but even then, a high output V-6 could do for the H3 what the Vortec V-8 did for the heavier H2 in lieu of the turbodiesel found in the H1. That both the H2 and a vehicle like the Terracross can be considered a rel-ative of the H1 is testament to the flexibility of the Hummer concept and bodes well for the future of this amazing nameplate.

INDEX

Other MBI Publishing Company titles of interest:

Four-Wheeler's Bible
ISBN 0-7603-1056-4

Corvette C5
ISBN 0-7603-0457-2

Porsche Boxster
ISBN 0-7603-0519-6

Mini Cooper
ISBN 0-7604-1157-9

The American Auto Factory
ISBN 0-7603-1059-9

Corvette: 50 Years
ISBN 0-7603-1180-3

Cannonball!
ISBN 0-7603-1090-4

Outlaw Sprints
ISBN 0-7603-1156-0

Harley-Davidson Century
ISBN 0-7603-1155-2

Find us on the internet at www.motorbooks.com   1-800-826-6600